THE
FALAFEL
COOKBOOK

HarperCollins*Publishers*
1 London Bridge Street
London SE1 9GF

HarperCollins*Publishers*
1st Floor, Watermarque Building, Ringsend Road
Dublin 4, Ireland

www.harpercollins.co.uk

First published by HarperCollins*Publishers* 2021

10 9 8 7 6 5 4 3 2 1

Text © HarperCollins*Publishers* 2021
Photography © Joff Lee 2021

Food Stylist: Mari Williams
Prop Stylist: Rebecca Newport

Heather Thomas asserts the moral right to be identified as the author of this work.

A catalogue record of this book is available from the British Library.

HB ISBN 978-0-00-840630-1
EB ISBN 978-0-00-840631-8

Printed and bound in Latvia

When using kitchen appliances, please always follow the manufacturer's instructions.

FSC™ is a non-profit international organisation established to promote the
responsible management of the world's forests. Products carrying the FSC
label are independently certified to assure consumers that they come from
forests that are managed to meet the social, economic and ecological needs
of present and future generations, and other controlled sources.

Find out more about HarperCollins and the environment at
www.harpercollins.co.uk/green

THE
FALAFEL
COOKBOOK

HEATHER THOMAS

HarperCollins*Publishers*

CONTENTS

//

INTRODUCTION

//

Golden and crispy on the outside, deliciously moist and fluffy inside, heady with spices and aromatic herbs, what's not to like about falafel? This simple, unpretentious street food has become increasingly popular as more of us are embracing a healthier diet and Mediterranean-style food.

Falafel are great for sharing and are beloved of meze platters. There is a growing trend away from complex recipes to simpler options and uncomplicated meals as we all become more mindful about what we eat. People are demanding more fresh and healthy plant-based food, and falafel fit the bill perfectly. They even have their own emoji and a Google Doodle on International Falafel Day on 12th June. And because they are entirely plant-based, economical and convenient, they are a very sustainable food and, made from chickpeas (garbanzo beans), are an excellent source of plant protein and a delicious substitute for meat.

VERSATILITY

Vegetarian eating is now mainstream as more people are switching to a completely meat-free diet. One of the great things about falafel is their universal appeal – to meat-eaters as well as vegetarians and vegans. Their versatility has been key to their success as they have moved beyond being a tasty fast-food snack with a slick of tahini that you can eat on-the-go, to a filling for pita pockets, sandwiches and wraps, tacos, burgers and sliders. They are even served as faux 'meat' in 'sausage' rolls and 'meatballs'. They can be made the traditional way from soaked chickpeas (garbanzo beans), or by using tinned chickpeas (garbanzo beans) combined with tasty root vegetables, such as beetroot and sweet potato. They can be coloured emerald green with herbs, spinach, kale and peas, or stuffed with halloumi or salty feta. Serve them in salads, as part of a meze platter with a selection of dips, sauces and pickles, or even in breakfast fritters and shakshuka.

NUTRITION AND HEALTH

Falafel are among the healthiest foods you can eat. They are a good source of protein, healthy carbs, vitamins B and C and a wide range of minerals. They are also high in soluble fibre, which boosts gut health and helps lower LDL (bad) blood cholesterol. They are low in fat (especially if you bake or shallow-fry them) and gluten-free if using chickpea (gram) flour. In addition, the spices and herbs in falafel contain antioxidants that prevent or delay damage to the cells in our bodies and help protect us against heart disease and cancer.

MAKING FALAFEL

Luckily for us, falafel are a breeze to make and the ultimate fast food. All you need to do is soak dried chickpeas (garbanzo beans) in water overnight, then grind them with herbs, spices, garlic, onion and flavourings, and shape them into little balls or patties before frying or baking until appetizingly crispy. You don't need any specialist skills or equipment apart from a large blender or food processor.

You will find an exciting range of recipes in this book, ranging from traditional dishes and accompaniments to snacks and street food, salads and substantial main courses. There are healthy recipes from Egypt, the Lebanon, Israel, Morocco, Turkey and Greece as well as India, Mexico, the Caribbean, Thailand and Italy. There's something for everyone, whether you're a meat-eater, a vegetarian or a vegan.

STORING AND FREEZING

You can keep falafel fresh in a sealed container in the fridge for up to three days.

To freeze cooked falafel, place them on a tray and freeze for 1 hour, then remove from the freezer and arrange them in a plastic container with wax paper between the layers. They will freeze well for up to one month.

To freeze uncooked falafel balls, place them on a tray and freeze for 1 hour, then place in a plastic container (as above) or a freezer bag. They will freeze well for up to three months.

REHEATING FALAFEL

To reheat cooked falafel, just shallow-fry them in oil over a medium heat for about 4–5 minutes until heated through, crisp and golden or bake them in a preheated oven at 180°C (160°C fan)/350°F/gas 4 for 15 minutes until hot and crisp on the outside.

Thaw frozen falafel in the fridge before baking, shallow-frying or microwaving them. Or you can reheat from frozen: just place on a baking tray (cookie sheet) and bake in a preheated oven at 180°C (160°C fan)/350°F/gas 4 for 15–20 minutes.

FLAVOURINGS

The flavourings you choose will make all the difference and can be transformational. You can choose from the following:

- **Spices:** the traditional spices for falafel include ground cumin and coriander, but you can also add ginger, cinnamon, turmeric, nutmeg, allspice, paprika and cayenne. For a more intense flavour, toast some cumin, coriander or fennel seeds and then grind them before adding to the falafel mixture. Or use diced or grated fresh root ginger.

- **Herbs:** the conventional herbs to use are oregano, marjoram, flat-leaf parsley, mint, dill and coriander (cilantro). Experiment with other herbs too, including basil, thyme and fennel.

- **Vegetables:** onions – white, red or spring onions (scallions) and shallots – all add flavour, as does garlic. Root vegetables are sometimes added for flavour, colour and sweetness, especially sweet potatoes, carrots, pumpkin and squash. Peas (fresh or frozen) and spinach colour falafel a lovely bright green.

- **Drizzles:** these are the finishing touches that make all the difference to flavour and appearance. You can add some spice and heat with harissa, hot sauce or sweet chilli sauce. Add sweetness with balsamic vinegar or glaze or pomegranate molasses. Be adventurous and drizzle with pesto or satay sauce, or be traditional and opt for a plain or lemony tahini sauce.

- **Dips and accompaniments:** the simplest accompaniment is a bowl of chilled yoghurt swirled with harissa paste, flavoured with lemon zest or sprinkled with herbs. Alternatively, try labneh, hummus, tzatziki, guacamole and tomato salsa. Pickled chillies, cucumber, beetroot (beets) and turnips also provide contrasting and complementary flavours. Serve with warm pita bread triangles or pockets, flatbreads, tortillas and wraps, or just some delicious crusty bread.

BASICS

TRADITIONAL FALAFEL

///

This is the basic traditional recipe for crispy falafel, although you can vary the spices and the size and shape of the balls. You must use soaked dried chickpeas (garbanzo beans) for this recipe. If you use the tinned sort they will not hold together so well and will have a totally different texture. If you use chickpea (gram) flour, the falafel will be gluten-free.

MAKES APPROX. 24 FALAFEL
SOAK OVERNIGHT
PREP 20 MINUTES
CHILL 1–2 HOURS (OPTIONAL)
COOK 10–15 MINUTES

300g (10½oz/generous 1¼ cups) chickpeas (garbanzo beans) (dried weight)
1 small onion, chopped
a bunch of flat-leaf parsley, chopped
4 garlic cloves, crushed
1½ tbsp chickpea (gram) flour
1 tsp baking powder
1 tsp sea salt
1 tsp ground cumin
1 tsp ground coriander
¼ tsp ground ginger
a good pinch of cayenne pepper
sunflower or vegetable oil, for frying
freshly ground black pepper

Put the chickpeas in a large bowl and cover with at least twice as much cold water. You will need plenty as the chickpeas swell and double in size. Leave to soak overnight. The following day, drain the chickpeas and pat dry with kitchen paper (paper towels).

Tip the chickpeas into a food processor and blitz with the onion, parsley and garlic. Add the chickpea flour, baking powder, salt and spices. Pulse, scraping down the sides occasionally, until everything is well combined, finely chopped and the mixture holds together. If it's too dry and falls apart, add 2–3 tablespoons cold water. Add a good grinding of black pepper and blitz again. Take care not to over-process – the texture should be coarse.

Take a spoonful of the falafel mixture and, with damp hands, shape it into a small ball. Repeat with the remaining mixture. If preferred, you can flatten the balls slightly to form patties (these may be a better shape if you are using the falafel in wraps or sandwiches). If wished, cover and chill in the fridge for 1–2 hours. This will help them stay together when you fry them.

Pour the oil into a deep heavy-based saucepan to a depth of at least 7.5cm (3in). Place over a medium to high heat and when the temperature reaches 180°C (350°F) (you can use a sugar thermometer to check), add the falafel, a few at a time, being careful not to overcrowd the pan. Fry for 4–5 minutes until crisp and golden brown all over, then remove with a slotted spoon and drain on kitchen paper.

Serve piping hot or leave to cool and add to salads, wraps and sandwiches.

REALLY GREEN FALAFEL

//

These golden falafel look so pretty when you bite into them and discover the bright green interior. Packed with fresh herbs and spices, they are crispy on the outside and moist inside. Try them and see.

MAKES APPROX. 24 FALAFEL
SOAK OVERNIGHT
PREP 20 MINUTES
CHILL 1–2 HOURS (OPTIONAL)
COOK 10–15 MINUTES

300g (10½oz/generous 1¼ cups)
   chickpeas (garbanzo beans)
   (dried weight)
6 spring onions (scallions), sliced
a bunch of coriander (cilantro),
   chopped
a bunch of flat-leaf parsley,
   chopped
a handful of mint, finely chopped
4 garlic cloves, crushed
1½ tbsp chickpea (gram) flour
1 tsp baking powder
1 tsp ground cumin
1 tsp ground coriander
½ tsp ground cardamom
a good pinch of cayenne pepper
1 tsp sea salt
sunflower or vegetable oil,
   for frying
freshly ground black pepper

Put the chickpeas in a large bowl and cover with at least twice as much cold water. Leave to soak overnight. The following day, drain the chickpeas and pat dry with kitchen paper (paper towels).

Transfer the chickpeas to a food processor and blitz with the spring onions, herbs and garlic. Add the chickpea flour, baking powder, spices and salt. Pulse, scraping down the sides occasionally, until everything is well combined, finely chopped and the mixture holds together. If it's too dry and falls apart, add 2–3 tablespoons cold water. Add a good grinding of black pepper and blitz again. Take care not to over-process – the texture should be coarse.

Take a spoonful of the falafel mixture and, with damp hands, shape it into a small ball. Repeat with the remaining mixture. If preferred, you can flatten the balls slightly to form patties (these may be a better shape if you are using the falafel in wraps or sandwiches). If wished, cover them and chill in the fridge for 1–2 hours. This will help them stay together when you fry them.

Pour the oil into a deep heavy-based saucepan to a depth of at least 7.5cm (3in). Place over a medium to high heat and when the temperature reaches 180°C (350°F) (you can use a sugar thermometer to check), add the falafel, a few at a time, being careful not to overcrowd the pan. Fry for 4–5 minutes until crisp and golden brown all over, then remove with a slotted spoon and drain on kitchen paper.

Serve piping hot or leave to cool and add to salads, wraps and sandwiches.

VARIATIONS
· Add a chopped jalapeño pepper or a fresh green chilli.
· Try adding a little grated lemon zest.

CARROT AND CORIANDER FALAFEL

//

These speedy falafel patties are made with tinned chickpeas (garbanzo beans), so the texture is different from that of the traditional deep-fried ones (see page 14), which use soaked dried chickpeas. Handle them carefully when frying to prevent them falling apart.

MAKES 12 FALAFEL
PREP 20 MINUTES
CHILL 30 MINUTES
COOK 10–15 MINUTES

100g (3½oz) carrots, finely grated
400g (14oz) tin (1½ cups) chickpeas (garbanzo beans), rinsed and drained
1 small green chilli, deseeded and diced
1 garlic clove, crushed
grated zest of 1 lemon
a bunch of coriander (cilantro), finely chopped
1 tbsp plain (all-purpose) flour
½ tsp baking powder
½ tsp sea salt
a pinch of freshly ground black pepper
1 tsp cumin seeds
1 tsp coriander seeds
vegetable oil or sunflower oil, for shallow frying

Squeeze any excess moisture out of the carrot and pat dry with kitchen paper (paper towels) along with the drained chickpeas. Transfer to a food processor with the chilli, garlic, lemon zest, coriander, flour, baking powder and seasoning.

Dry-fry the cumin and coriander seeds in a small pan over a medium heat for 1–2 minutes or until they release their aroma. Remove immediately before they burn and add to the food processor.

Blitz until everything is well combined and you have a coarse paste that sticks together. Divide the mixture into 12 equal-sized portions and shape each one into a small ball. Flatten the balls slightly with your hands. Cover and chill in the fridge for at least 30 minutes to firm them up.

Heat the oil in a large non-stick frying pan (skillet) over a medium to high heat and, when it's hot, add the falafel in batches. Cook for about 2 minutes each side or until crisp and golden brown. Remove from the pan and drain on kitchen paper (paper towels). Serve immediately.

VARIATIONS
· Use fresh basil or flat-leaf parsley instead of the coriander (cilantro).
· If you don't have seeds, use the ground spices instead.
· Coat with sesame seeds before frying.

BEETROOT FALAFEL

//

These crisply fried falafel have a wonderful deep crimson colour and natural sweetness.
They are great in salads or added to pita pockets, wraps, flatbreads and sandwiches.
Serve them with yoghurt or tahini sauce.

MAKES 12 FALAFEL
PREP 20 MINUTES
CHILL 30 MINUTES
COOK 12–16 MINUTES

400g (14oz) tin (1½ cups)
   chickpeas (garbanzo beans),
   rinsed and drained
½ red onion, grated
3 garlic cloves, crushed
2 carrots, grated
75g (2½oz) raw beetroot (beets),
   grated
1–2 tsp harissa paste
1 tsp ground cumin
1 tsp ground coriander
1 tsp sea salt
75g (2½oz/1 cup) chickpea
   (gram) flour
½ tsp baking powder
sesame seeds, for coating
olive oil, for frying

Pat dry the drained chickpeas with kitchen paper (paper towels) and put them into a large food processor with the onion, garlic, carrot, beetroot, harissa paste, ground spices, sea salt, flour and baking powder. Pulse until you have a thick coarse paste – it should not be too smooth.

Divide the mixture into 12 portions and, using your hands, mould each one into a ball. Press down gently to flatten it into a patty.

Spread out some sesame seeds on a plate and lightly press the falafel into them until coated on both sides. Cover and chill in the fridge for 30 minutes to firm them up.

Pour enough oil into a large non-stick frying pan (skillet) to just cover the base and set over a medium to high heat. When the oil is hot, add the falafel, a few at a time, and fry for 6–8 minutes, turning halfway through, until crisp and lightly browned on both sides. Serve immediately.

VARIATIONS
• Try rose harissa – the rose petals and rose water add sweetness and soften the heat of the paste.
• If you don't have harissa, you could add some dried chilli flakes instead.
• Omit the carrots and add more beetroot (beets).

WINTER CHESTNUT FALAFEL

//

Made with sweet potato, chestnuts and cranberries, these gently spiced falafel are great to serve at festive parties and Christmas dinners. Serve with cranberry sauce, redcurrant jelly, spicy fruit chutney or with a bowl of yoghurt swirled with pomegranate molasses.

MAKES APPROX. 18 FALAFEL
SOAK OVERNIGHT
PREP 20 MINUTES
CHILL 1–2 HOURS (OPTIONAL)
COOK 1 HOUR

225g (8oz/1 cup) chickpeas (garbanzo beans) (dried weight)

1 large sweet potato, washed and scrubbed

a handful of flat-leaf parsley, chopped

2 garlic cloves, crushed

100g (3½oz/1 cup) vacuum-packed chestnuts

3–4 tbsp chickpea (gram) flour

1 tsp baking powder

1 tsp sea salt

1 tsp ground cumin

½ tsp ground nutmeg

¼ tsp ground cinnamon

50g (2oz/½ cup) fresh cranberries

sunflower or vegetable oil, for frying

freshly ground black pepper

Put the chickpeas in a large bowl and cover with at least twice as much cold water. You will need plenty as the chickpeas swell and double in size. Leave to soak overnight. The following day, drain the chickpeas and pat dry with kitchen paper (paper towels).

Preheat the oven to 200°C (180°C fan)/400°F/gas 6 and bake the sweet potato for 45–50 minutes until soft. When it's cool enough to handle, cut it open and scoop out the flesh. Mash coarsely. Alternatively, cook in the microwave.

Tip the chickpeas into a food processor and blitz for 1 minute. Scrape down the sides and add the sweet potato, parsley, garlic and chestnuts. Pulse until well combined and roughly chopped.

Add the chickpea flour, baking powder, salt and spices. Pulse, scraping down the sides of the processor occasionally, until everything is finely chopped and the mixture holds together. If it's too dry and falls apart, add a little cold water. If it's too loose, add another spoonful or so of flour. Add a good grinding of black pepper and pulse briefly. Lastly, mix in the cranberries, distributing them throughout the mixture.

Take a tablespoonful of the falafel mixture and, with damp hands, shape it into a ball. Repeat with the remaining mixture. If preferred, you can flatten the balls slightly to form patties (these may be a better shape if you are using the falafel in wraps or sandwiches). If wished, cover them and chill in the fridge for 1–2 hours until you're ready to cook. This will also firm them up before frying.

Pour the oil into a deep heavy-based saucepan to a depth of at least 7.5cm (3in). Place over a medium to high heat and when the temperature reaches 180°C (350°F) (you can use a sugar thermometer to check), add the falafel, a few at a time, being careful not to overcrowd the pan. Fry for 4–5 minutes until crisp and golden brown all over, then remove with a slotted spoon and drain on kitchen paper (paper towels). Serve piping hot.

Tip: Take care not to over-process the falafel mixture – it should have a slightly coarse grainy texture and should not be smooth like hummus.

VARIATIONS
- You can use peeled cooked chestnuts instead of vacuum-packed ones.
- Add some grated orange or clementine zest.

OVEN-BAKED VEGGIE FALAFEL

//

To purists, making falafel with tinned chickpeas (garbanzo beans) and baking them in the oven is heresy. However, for busy people in a hurry, there's no overnight soaking or deep- or shallow-frying and there are added green vegetables to make them an easy healthy option.

MAKES 12 FALAFEL
PREP 20 MINUTES
COOK 25–30 MINUTES

400g (14oz) tin (1½ cups) chickpeas (garbanzo beans), rinsed and drained
a small bunch of spring onions (scallions), sliced
3 garlic cloves, crushed
75g (2½oz/2 cups) washed, trimmed and shredded spinach
100g (3½oz) broccoli florets
150g (5½oz/1 cup) frozen peas, defrosted
a bunch of basil or coriander (cilantro), chopped
½ tsp ground cumin
1 tbsp tahini
a squeeze of lemon juice
½ tsp baking powder
1–2 tbsp plain (all-purpose) flour
olive or sunflower oil, for brushing
sea salt and freshly ground black pepper

Preheat the oven to 220°C (200°C fan)/425°F/gas 7. Line a large baking tray (cookie sheet) with baking parchment.

Pat dry the drained chickpeas with kitchen paper (paper towels) and put them into a large food processor with the spring onions, garlic, spinach, broccoli, peas, herbs, cumin, tahini, lemon juice and baking powder. Pulse until the mixture is well combined and everything is coarsely chopped.

Transfer to a large bowl and stir in enough flour to bind the mixture to a coarse paste that sticks together. Season with salt and pepper. Divide the mixture into 12 equal-sized portions and shape each one into a ball. Flatten the balls slightly with your hands to make patties.

Lightly brush the patties with oil and place them on the lined baking tray. Bake in the preheated oven for 25–30 minutes, turning them over halfway through, until crisp and golden brown. Serve immediately.

VARIATIONS
· Add some bottled or tinned jalapeño peppers.
· Top with guacamole or soured cream.

PUMPKIN OR SQUASH FALAFEL

//

These falafel are nice to make in the autumn when pumpkin and squash are in season and plentiful. They add natural sweetness to the spicy mixture. Serve with warm pita triangles, tahini sauce or yoghurt feta sauce.

MAKES APPROX. 24 FALAFEL
SOAK OVERNIGHT
PREP 20 MINUTES
CHILL 1–2 HOURS (OPTIONAL)
COOK 12–15 MINUTES

300g (10½oz/generous 1¼ cups) chickpeas (garbanzo beans) (dried weight)
225g (8oz) pumpkin or butternut squash, peeled, deseeded and chopped
½ red onion, chopped
a handful of coriander (cilantro), chopped
2 garlic cloves, crushed
3 tbsp chickpea (gram) flour
1 tsp baking powder
1 tsp sea salt
1 tsp ground cumin
1 tsp ground coriander
½ tsp ground cinnamon
¼ tsp hot paprika
sunflower or vegetable oil, for frying
freshly ground black pepper

Put the chickpeas in a large bowl and cover with at least twice as much cold water. You will need plenty as the chickpeas swell and double in size. Leave to soak overnight. The following day, drain the chickpeas and pat dry with kitchen paper (paper towels).

Tip the chickpeas into a food processor and blitz for 1 minute. Scrape down the sides and add the pumpkin or squash, onion, coriander and garlic. Pulse until well combined and roughly chopped.

Add the chickpea flour, baking powder, salt and spices. Pulse, scraping down the sides of the processor occasionally, until everything is finely chopped and the mixture holds together. If it's too dry and falls apart, add 2–3 tablespoons cold water. If it's too loose, add another spoonful of flour. Add a good grinding of black pepper and blitz again. Take care not to over-process – the falafel should have a grainy texture and should not be smooth like hummus.

Take a spoonful of the falafel mixture and, with damp hands, shape it into a ball. Repeat with the remaining mixture. If preferred, you can flatten the balls slightly to form patties (these may be a better shape if you are using the falafel in wraps or sandwiches). If wished, cover them and chill in the fridge for 1–2 hours until you're ready to cook.

Pour the oil into a deep heavy-based saucepan to a depth of at least 7.5cm (3 in). Place over a medium to high heat and when the temperature reaches 180°C (350°F) (you can use a sugar thermometer to check), add the falafel, a few at a time, being careful not to overcrowd the pan. Fry for 4–5 minutes until crisp and golden brown all over, then remove with a slotted spoon and drain on kitchen paper. Serve piping hot.

SPINACH AND CHILLI FALAFEL

//

Adding spinach to a basic falafel mix gives the crisply fried balls a fresh green colour. If you don't want to deep-fry the falafel, just flatten the patties and shallow-fry them in a large frying pan (skillet).

MAKES APPROX. 24 FALAFEL
SOAK OVERNIGHT
PREP 20 MINUTES
COOK 10–15 MINUTES

300g (10½oz/generous 1¼ cups) chickpeas (garbanzo beans) (dried weight)
1 small onion, chopped
a bunch of flat-leaf parsley, chopped
4 garlic cloves, crushed
75g (2½oz/2 cups) chopped spinach leaves
1 fresh red chilli, diced
1½ tbsp chickpea (gram) flour
1 tsp baking powder
1 tsp sea salt
1 tsp ground cumin
½ tsp ground coriander
sunflower or vegetable oil, for frying

Put the chickpeas in a large bowl and cover with plenty of cold water. Leave to soak overnight. The following day, drain the chickpeas and pat dry with kitchen paper (paper towels).

Tip the chickpeas into a food processor and blitz with the onion, parsley, garlic, spinach and chilli until coarsely chopped. Add the chickpea flour, baking powder, salt and ground spices. Pulse, scraping down the sides of the bowl occasionally, until everything is well combined and the mixture holds together. If it's too dry and falls apart, add 2–3 tablespoons cold water; too wet, add another spoonful of flour.

Take a spoonful of the falafel mixture and, with damp hands, shape it into a small ball. Repeat with the remaining mixture. If preferred, you can flatten the balls slightly to form patties

Pour the oil into a deep heavy-based saucepan to a depth of at least 7.5cm (3in). Place over a medium to high heat and when the temperature reaches 180°C (350°F) (use a sugar thermometer to check), add the falafel, a few at a time, being careful not to overcrowd the pan. Fry for 4–5 minutes until crisp and golden brown all over, then remove with a slotted spoon and drain on kitchen paper (paper towels). Serve piping hot.

VARIATIONS
· You can use plain (all-purpose) flour if you don't have chickpea (gram) flour.
· Add a spoonful of tahini to the mix.
· Use coriander (cilantro) or basil instead of parsley.
· If you don't have a fresh chilli, dried chilli flakes are OK.
· Add a dash of lemon juice and some grated zest.

QUICK-AND-EASY BUTTERBEAN FALAFEL

//

Baked falafel made with tinned butterbeans are lighter and quicker to make than the traditional sort. Serve these with a salad for a light lunch or flatten them slightly before cooking and use as a filling for warm pita 'pockets' or gyros. Drizzle with tahini sauce, yoghurt or even some sweet chilli sauce.

MAKES APPROX. 12 FALAFEL
PREP 15 MINUTES
COOK 15–20 MINUTES

1 courgette (zucchini), trimmed
   and sliced
a handful of spinach or curly kale,
   washed, trimmed and stalks
   removed
4 spring onions (scallions),
   chopped
2 garlic cloves, crushed
a handful of flat-leaf parsley,
   chopped
400g (14oz) tin (4 cups)
   butterbeans (lima beans),
   rinsed and drained
2 tbsp tahini
½ tsp ground coriander
½ tsp sweet paprika
½ tsp sea salt
1 tbsp chickpea (gram) flour
½ tsp baking powder
grated zest of 1 lemon
olive oil, for brushing
sesame seeds, for coating

Preheat the oven to 180°C (160°C fan)/350°F/gas 4. Line a baking tray (cookie sheet) with parchment paper.

Blitz the courgette, spinach or kale, spring onions, garlic and parsley in a food processor. Add the butterbeans, tahini, spices, salt, flour, baking powder and lemon zest. Blitz, stopping once or twice to scrape down the sides of the bowl, until well combined, finely chopped and firm. If the mixture is too sticky, add some more flour; if it's too dry, add a little water.

Take spoonfuls of the mixture and, using your hands, mould them into balls (the size of golf balls or ping pong balls). Brush lightly with oil and roll in the sesame seeds. Place on the baking tray.

Bake in the preheated oven for 15–20 minutes, turning them halfway through, until crisp and golden brown all over. Serve immediately.

VARIATIONS
· Use peanut butter instead of tahini.
· Vary the spices: try smoked paprika, ground cumin and cayenne pepper.
· Add some diced chilli.
· Use ½ red or white onion instead of spring onions (scallions).
· Use mint or coriander (cilantro) instead of parsley.

GREEN PEA

//

These falafel are an appetizing bright green inside. The peas add sweetness as well as protein, and they're very easy to make and cook. Eat them on their own with a dip or a tahini yoghurt drizzle or serve with salad, as part of a meze spread or in sandwiches, wraps and pita bread.

MAKES APPROX. 10 FALAFEL
PREP 20 MINUTES
COOK 8–12 MINUTES

400g (14oz) tin (1½ cups) chickpeas (garbanzo beans), rinsed and drained
150g (5½oz/1 cup) frozen peas, defrosted
½ onion, chopped
2 garlic cloves, crushed
a large handful of flat-leaf parsley
a large handful of mint
2 tbsp tahini
1 tsp ground cumin
½ tsp ground coriander
1 tsp sea salt
¼ tsp dried chilli flakes
grated zest of 1 lemon, plus a little lemon juice
2 tbsp chickpea (gram) flour
1 tsp baking powder
olive or sunflower oil, for frying

Pulse the chickpeas, peas, onion, garlic, herbs and tahini in a food processor until finely chopped.

Add the spices, salt, chilli flakes, lemon zest, flour and baking powder. Pulse until everything is well combined, firm and finely chopped. If it's too dry, add a little lemon juice or water. If it's too sticky, add some more flour.

Take spoonfuls of the mixture and shape, with your hands, into balls. Flatten them slightly into patties.

Heat the oil to a depth of about 2cm (1 inch) in a large non-stick frying pan (skillet) over a medium to high heat. When it's really hot, add a batch of falafel to the pan (don't overcrowd them) and cook for 2–3 minutes each side until crisp and golden brown. Remove and drain on kitchen paper (paper towels) while you cook the remaining falafel. Serve immediately.

VARIATIONS
· Use cooked fresh garden peas.
· Substitute peanut butter or cashew butter for the tahini.
· Use spring onions (scallions) or red onion.

SWEET POTATO FALAFEL

//

These falafel are unusual in so far as they don't contain any whole chickpeas (garbanzo beans). Because the mixture can be quite wet, chickpea (gram) flour is used to bind it together. They are quite delicate and you might find it helpful to mould them with two spoons, an ice cream scoop or even a special falafel maker scoop, which can be bought online.

MAKES APPROX. 12 FALAFEL
PREP 15 MINUTES
CHILL 30–45 MINUTES
COOK 1 HOUR

600g (1lb 5oz) sweet potatoes, washed and scrubbed
3 garlic cloves, crushed
1 tsp ground cumin
1 tsp ground coriander
1 tsp grated fresh root ginger
1 small red chilli, deseeded and diced
a handful of flat-leaf parsley, finely chopped
115g (4oz/1½ cups) chickpea (gram) flour
oil, for greasing
sea salt and freshly ground black pepper

Preheat the oven to 200°C (180°C fan)/400°F/gas 6.

Put the sweet potatoes on a baking tray (cookie sheet) and roast in the preheated oven for 45–50 minutes until tender. Set aside until they are cool enough to handle. Alternatively, cook in the microwave.

Cut the sweet potatoes in half and, with a spoon, scoop out the flesh. Place in a bowl with the garlic, ground spices, ginger, chilli, parsley and flour. Season with salt and pepper and then mash everything together with a potato masher.

Cover the bowl and chill in the fridge for 30–45 minutes to firm up the mixture. Remove and, with your hands, take spoonfuls of the mixture and shape into balls. Flatten them slightly and place, slightly apart, on a lightly oiled baking tray.

Bake in the preheated oven for 10–15 minutes or until the falafel are crisp and golden brown.

Tip: This is a great way to use up leftover cooked sweet potatoes.

VARIATIONS
- Add some grated lemon zest and juice.
- Use coriander (cilantro) instead of parsley.
- Sprinkle the falafel with sesame seeds before baking.

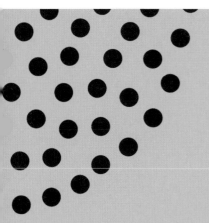

ACCOMPANIMENTS

YOGHURT FETA SAUCE

//

This simple sauce is a delicious accompaniment for hot falafel. You can also use it as a salad dressing or to drizzle over roasted vegetables. Don't be tempted to add salt – the feta is salty enough without any extra help from you!

**MAKES APPROX. 400ML
(14FL OZ/1½ CUPS)
PREP 10 MINUTES
CHILL 1 HOUR**

175g (6oz) feta cheese
240g (8½oz/1 cup) Greek
   yoghurt
1 garlic clove, crushed
a small handful of mint, chopped
a few sprigs of coriander
   (cilantro), finely chopped
grated zest and juice of ½ lemon
freshly ground black pepper

Break the feta into a bowl and mash it with a fork. Stir in the yoghurt and garlic and mix well.

Add the chopped herbs together with the grated lemon zest and juice. Season to taste with a grinding of black pepper and thin with cold water to the desired consistency.

Cover and chill in the fridge for at least 1 hour to enhance the flavours. This will keep well in a sealed container in the fridge for up to 2 days.

VARIATIONS
· Vary the herbs: try basil, dill, flat-leaf parsley or chives.
· Add a mashed avocado to the sauce.
· Add a pinch of dried oregano.
· Make the sauce a silkier consistency by adding a spoonful of olive oil.

QUICK-AND-EASY HUMMUS

//

Traditionally, hummus is made by soaking chickpeas (garbanzo beans) overnight before cooking and blending them with tahini and garlic to a rough purée. However, using tinned saves time and most people can't tell the difference. Serve this with falafel, as a dip, a topping for bread or warm pita, a filling for sandwiches and wraps, or a base for roasted vegetables and grilled meat or chicken.

**MAKES APPROX. 500G
(1LB 2OZ/3 CUPS)
PREP 15 MINUTES**

2 x 400g (14oz) tins (3 cups) chickpeas (garbanzo beans)
4 tbsp tahini
3–4 garlic cloves, crushed
1 tbsp extra-virgin olive oil, plus extra for drizzling
juice of 1 large lemon, plus extra for drizzling
fine sea salt crystals
finely chopped parsley, for sprinkling
za'atar, paprika or sumac, for dusting

Drain the tinned chickpeas over a bowl, reserving the liquid, and rinse them under running cold water.

Pat dry with kitchen paper (paper towels) and blitz in a food processor with the tahini, garlic, olive oil and lemon juice.

Add some of the reserved chickpea liquid (aquafaba) or extra oil or lemon juice until you end up with the consistency you want. The hummus should be quite soft (but not runny) and a little grainy, but not too smooth. Season to taste with salt.

Transfer to a serving bowl and sprinkle with parsley. Drizzle with olive oil and more lemon juice, if desired, and dust with za'atar, paprika or sumac. It will keep well in a sealed container in the fridge for up to 3 days.

VARIATIONS
- Top with chopped raw or caramelized red onions and pine nuts.
- Sprinkle with pomegranate seeds.
- Blitz with a roasted red pepper.
- Add some coriander (cilantro), parsley or basil.
- Add diced fresh chilli, dried chilli flakes or a swirl of harissa paste.
- Sprinkle with dukkah or toasted fennel, cumin, pumpkin and coriander seeds.
- Make it creamier by stirring in some Greek yoghurt.

SKORDALIA

//

This intensely garlicky mixture pops up on menus all over Greece. It can be used as a dip, thinned as a sauce or drizzle, or served as an accompaniment for falafel. Skordalia is very quick and easy to make – a great way of using up stale bread.

MAKES APPROX. 350G (12OZ/ GENEROUS 1 CUP)
SOAK 5 MINUTES
PREP 10 MINUTES

150g (5½oz/3 slices) stale white bread, crusts removed
6 garlic cloves, peeled
½ tsp sea salt crystals
85g (3oz/½ cup) blanched almonds
1 tbsp red wine vinegar
120ml (4fl oz/½ cup) fruity extra-virgin olive oil
a splash of lemon juice
sea salt and freshly ground black pepper

Put the bread in a bowl, over with cold water and set aside to soak for 5 minutes. Remove the bread and gently squeeze out any surplus water.

Put the garlic cloves and sea salt in a pestle and mortar and grind to a paste.

Pulse the soaked bread, garlic paste, almonds and vinegar in a food processor until smooth. With the motor running, gradually add the olive oil in a thin, steady stream through the feed tube until the skordalia is thick and grainy. Season to taste with salt and pepper and add a splash of lemon juice.

If you want to use the skordalia as a sauce or drizzle, thin it to the desired consistency by stirring in a little water.

Tip: To blanch almonds, just add them to a pan of boiling water and boil for 1 minute. Drain and cool the almonds under running cold water. Pat dry and slip off their skins between your fingers. Squeeze gently and the almonds will pop out.

VARIATIONS
· Use a handful of pine nuts instead of almonds.
· Swirl in some pomegranate molasses.

LABNEH

///

This dense soft cheese is made from strained Greek yoghurt. It's a great accompaniment for falafel or you can serve it as a dip, add it to wraps and pita or use as a delicious spread for crusty bread. And it's really healthy and a good source of protein and probiotics.

MAKES 480G (1LB 1OZ/ 2 CUPS)
PREP 10 MINUTES
DRAIN 24 HOURS

480g (1lb 1oz/2 cups) thick full-fat Greek yoghurt
½ tsp sea salt flakes
extra-virgin olive oil, for drizzling
za'atar, for sprinkling

Line a sieve with a large square of cheesecloth (muslin cloth) and set over a bowl.

Mix the yoghurt with the sea salt and spoon into the centre of the cheesecloth. Gather up the sides to enclose the yoghurt tightly and tie in a bow or knot at the top. Alternatively, tie with kitchen string.

Chill in the fridge for 24 hours before removing it and untying the cheesecloth. Throw away any liquid in the bowl and place the drained labneh in a serving bowl.

Serve the labneh at room temperature, drizzled with olive oil and sprinkled with za'atar. It will stay fresh for up to 1 week if you keep it in a sealed container in the fridge.

VARIATIONS
- Drizzle with clear Greek honey instead of olive oil.
- Top with dukkah, dried chilli or Aleppo red pepper flakes, roasted fennel or cumin seeds.
- Stir in some chopped mint, dill or cilantro (coriander).
- Add some crushed garlic.

TZATZIKI

//

Refreshing and cooling, tzatziki is eaten throughout the Middle East, Turkey and Greece. It's the perfect accompaniment to falafel – as a dip, a sauce or even a salad dressing in pita, wraps and gyros. If you're in a hurry you can just dice the cucumber without deseeding and draining it, but it won't taste so authentic or good. Vegans can use dairy-free yoghurt.

**MAKES APPROX. 300G
(10½OZ/1¼ CUPS)
PREP 15 MINUTES
DRAIN 30 MINUTES
CHILL 1 HOUR**

½ large cucumber
a good pinch of sea salt
240g (8½oz/1 cup) Greek
   yoghurt
3 garlic cloves, crushed
1 tbsp fruity extra-virgin olive oil
grated zest and juice of ½ lemon
a few sprigs of mint, finely
   chopped
a few sprigs of dill, finely chopped
finely ground sea salt
freshly ground black pepper

Cut the cucumber in half lengthways and carefully scoop out the seeds with a small spoon. Cut the cucumber into small dice and place them in a colander. Sprinkle them with a good pinch of sea salt and set aside to drain for at least 30 minutes.

Squeeze out any liquid from the cucumber with your hands and then pat dry with kitchen paper (paper towels).

In a bowl, mix together the yoghurt, garlic, olive oil, lemon zest and juice, and herbs. Stir in the drained cucumber and season to taste with salt and black pepper.

Cover the bowl and chill in the fridge for at least an hour.

VARIATIONS
- Use 2 teaspoons red wine vinegar instead of lemon juice.
- Add some toasted crushed fennel seeds and diced fennel bulb.
- Stir in some chopped spinach, watercress or rocket (arugula).
- Add diced red beetroot (beets) for a sweeter, delicately pink tzatziki.

AVOCADO TAHINI DIP

//

This lovely green dip can be served with falafel, warm pita, raw vegetable crudités or tortilla chips. For a chunkier texture, mix by hand and mash the avocado coarsely before adding. Vegans can use dairy-free yoghurt.

**MAKES APPROX. 300G
(10½OZ/1¼ CUPS)
PREP 15 MINUTES
COOK 1–2 MINUTES**

250g (9oz) spinach, washed and
  trimmed
120g (4oz/½ cup) tahini
2 garlic cloves, crushed
½ tsp sea salt
a handful of chopped coriander
  (cilantro)
¼ tsp ground cumin
juice of 1 large lemon
2 ripe avocados, peeled and
  stoned (pitted)
120g (4oz/½ cup) thick Greek
  yoghurt

Put the wet spinach leaves in a large saucepan over a medium heat. Cover and cook for 2 minutes, shaking the pan occasionally, until the spinach wilts and turns bright green. Drain in a colander and press down well with a saucer to extract all the liquid. Pat dry with kitchen paper (paper towels) and chop.

Put the spinach in a food processor with the tahini, garlic and salt and pulse until well combined. Add the coriander, cumin, lemon juice and avocado flesh and pulse until smooth.

Add the yoghurt to loosen the dip and make it creamier. Pulse again and check the seasoning, adding more salt if necessary. If it's too thick, just add a little cold water to thin it.

Transfer to a serving bowl and serve immediately or cover with cling film (plastic wrap) and chill in the fridge for a few hours.

VARIATIONS
· Use curly kale, baby spinach leaves or rocket (arugula).
· Add 1–2 tablespoons olive oil for a creamier dip.
· Mix with Labneh (see page 35) instead of yoghurt.

TAHINI YOGHURT SAUCE

//

You can use this simple sauce as a salad dressing, a drizzle or even a dip. As you'll see from the variations below, it's extremely versatile, so just add your own flavourings. Vegans can make it with dairy-free yoghurt.

MAKES 240G (8½OZ/1 CUP)
PREP 10 MINUTES

1–2 garlic cloves, peeled
a good pinch of sea salt crystals
4 tbsp tahini
juice of 1 small lemon
240g (8½oz/1 cup) full-fat Greek
   yoghurt
freshly ground black pepper

Crush the garlic cloves and salt in a pestle and mortar.

Mix with the tahini and lemon juice in a bowl and stir in the yoghurt. Season to taste with black pepper. If wished, thin with cold water to the desired consistency.

Cover and store in an airtight container in the fridge for up to 2 days.

VARIATIONS
- Add ½ teaspoon ground cumin.
- Sprinkle with dried chilli flakes.
- Add some crushed dry-roasted seeds, e.g. cumin, coriander, sesame or nigella.
- Swirl in a little harissa or pomegranate molasses.
- For a silky finish, stir in a teaspoon of extra-virgin olive oil.
- Add chopped fresh herbs: Greek basil, dill, flat-leaf parsley, coriander (cilantro) or oregano.
- Stir in ½ teaspoon ground turmeric for a golden sauce.

LEMONY GREEN TAHINI SAUCE

//

This intensely green zingy sauce is perfect for serving with falafel. It's simple to make and keeps well in the fridge for up to three days. It's also a great accompaniment for roast chicken and lamb or griddled vegetables. If you omit the water you can use it as a dressing for pasta or even as a dip.

**MAKES APPROX. 480ML
(16FL OZ/2 CUPS)
PREP 15 MINUTES**

a bunch of flat-leaf parsley,
    roughly chopped
a bunch of coriander (cilantro),
    roughly chopped
2 garlic cloves, crushed
1 tsp sea salt
175g (6oz/¾ cup) tahini
juice of 1 lemon
3 tbsp extra-virgin olive oil
120ml (4fl oz/½ cup) cold water

Put the herbs, garlic and salt in a food processor and blitz to a green purée.

Add the tahini, lemon juice and olive oil and blitz until thick, smooth and well combined.

With the motor running, gradually add the water through the feed tube until you have the desired consistency.

Store in an airtight container in the fridge for up to 3 days.

VARIATIONS
· Add a fresh green chilli.
· Use 2 limes instead of a lemon.
· Vary the herbs: try fresh mint or basil.
· Add some ground cumin, coriander, sumac or za'atar.

LIGHT MEALS

MEXICAN FALAFEL TACOS

//

The key to easy taco making is to prepare the different salsas, sauces and drizzles in advance. You can even cheat and buy ready-made salsa and guacamole. For a Mexican flavour, we suggest adding ancho chilli powder to the falafel mixture before cooking it. However, you can use any falafel in this recipe.

SERVES 4
PREP 20–30 MINUTES
COOK 15–20 MINUTES IF
MAKING FRESH FALAFEL

1 quantity uncooked Traditional
   falafel mixture (see page 14)
1 tsp ancho chilli powder
sunflower or vegetable oil, for
   frying
100g (3½oz/scant ½ cup) tinned
   sweetcorn kernels
240g (8½oz/1 cup) tomato salsa
1 ripe avocado, peeled and stoned
   (pitted)
1 green chilli, diced
8 crisp taco shells
1 small cos (romaine) lettuce,
   shredded
a large handful of coriander
   (cilantro), chopped
lime wedges, for squeezing

LIME SOURED CREAM
240ml (8fl oz/1 cup) soured
   cream
1 tsp toasted cumin seeds,
   crushed
grated zest and juice of 2 limes
a few sprigs of coriander
   (cilantro), finely chopped
sea salt crystals

Make the lime soured cream: whisk all the ingredients together in a bowl, adding salt to taste. Cover and chill in the fridge until needed.

Make the falafel mixture according to the instructions in the recipe, adding the ancho chilli powder. Shape into small balls.

Pour the oil into a deep heavy-based saucepan to a depth of at least 7.5cm (3in). Place over a medium to high heat and when the temperature reaches 180°C (350°F) (you can use a sugar thermometer to check), add the falafel, a few at a time, being careful not to overcrowd the pan. Fry for 4–5 minutes until crisp and golden brown all over, then remove with a slotted spoon and drain on kitchen paper (paper towels).

Stir the sweetcorn kernels into the tomato salsa. Mash the avocado with the chilli.

Warm the taco shells in a low oven and fill them with the lettuce, mashed avocado and corn salsa. Divide the falafel among the shells and drizzle with the lime soured cream. Sprinkle with coriander and serve immediately with lime wedges for squeezing over.

Tip: To toast the cumin seeds, dry-fry them in a small frying pan (skillet) over a medium to high heat, tossing occasionally, for 1–2 minutes until fragrant and golden brown. Remove immediately.

VARIATIONS
· Sprinkle the tacos with grated mature Cheddar cheese.
· Drizzle with hot chilli sauce.
· Use guacamole instead of the mashed avocado.
· Add some black beans or refried beans.
· Use fennel or coriander seeds in the lime cream.

SPICED FALAFEL AND FETA BURGERS

//

A different take on falafel is to shape the mixture into burgers rather than the usual small balls.
These delicious veggie burgers make a quick-and-easy lunch served with salad.

SERVES 4
PREP 15 MINUTES
COOK 20 MINUTES

3 tbsp olive oil
1 large onion, finely chopped
2 garlic cloves, crushed
2 x 400g (14oz) tins (3 cups)
  chickpeas (garbanzo beans),
  rinsed and drained
150g (5½oz) feta cheese,
  crumbled
50g (2oz) sun-dried or sun-blush
  tomatoes, drained
a small bunch of coriander
  (cilantro)
grated zest of 1 lemon
1 tsp ground cumin
½ tsp ground coriander
1 medium free-range egg, beaten
chickpea (gram) flour, for binding
  (optional)
4 wholemeal rolls or seeded
  burger buns
shredded lettuce and sliced
  tomato
120g (4oz/½ cup) Tzatziki
  (see page 38)
chilli sauce or harissa (optional)
freshly ground black pepper

Heat 2 tablespoons of the olive oil in a frying pan (skillet) and cook the onion and garlic, stirring occasionally, over a low to medium heat for 10 minutes until softened but not coloured.

Transfer to a food processor and add the chickpeas, feta, tomatoes, coriander, lemon zest, spices and some of the beaten egg. Blitz until well-blended but still slightly coarse – the mixture should not be too smooth. If it's too dry, add more beaten egg; too wet, add a little chickpea (gram) flour. Season with black pepper.

Divide the mixture into four equal-sized portions and, with your hands, shape each one into a burger.

Heat the remaining olive oil in a large non-stick frying pan over a medium heat. Cook the burgers for 4–5 minutes each side, until lightly browned and heated right through.

Split the rolls or burger buns in half and lightly toast, if wished. Place some lettuce and tomato on the bases and add the hot burgers. Top with tzatziki and some chilli sauce or harissa if you want to add a little heat. Cover and serve immediately.

VARIATIONS
· Use flat-leaf parsley or basil.
· Add diced chilli or dried chilli flakes to the burger mix.
· Serve with fresh tomato salsa or mango chutney.
· Drizzle with pomegranate molasses, green pesto or some
  tomato ketchup.
· Add some sliced red onion rings to the salad in the rolls.

MUSHROOM FALAFEL

//

Mushrooms make an unusual but delicious addition to falafel. We've baked these ones, but you could shallow-fry them, if preferred. Pop them in warm pita pockets with tzatziki or for a more substantial meal, serve them hot in a tomato sauce with pasta, rice or quinoa.

SERVES 4
PREP 20 MINUTES
COOK 20–25 MINUTES

200g (7oz) white mushrooms, chopped
4 spring onions (scallions), chopped
3 garlic cloves, crushed
100g (3½oz) spinach, washed, trimmed, dried and shredded
a large handful of flat-leaf parsley, chopped
400g (14oz) tin (1½ cups) chickpeas (garbanzo beans), rinsed and drained
1 tsp sweet paprika
½ tsp ground cumin
½ tsp sea salt
2 tbsp tahini
1 tbsp olive oil, plus extra for brushing
juice of ½ lemon
1–2 tbsp chickpea (gram) flour
sesame seeds, for coating
green pesto, warm pita breads and salad, to serve

Preheat the oven to 200°C (180°C fan)/400°F/gas 6. Line a baking tray (cookie sheet) with baking parchment.

Pulse the mushrooms in a food processor until finely chopped. Transfer to a large mixing bowl.

Put the spring onions, garlic, spinach and parsley in the food processor and pulse until coarsely chopped. Pat the drained chickpeas dry with kitchen paper (paper towels) and add to the processor with the spices and salt. Blitz to a coarse paste, then tip into the mixing bowl and mix gently with the mushrooms.

Add the tahini, olive oil and lemon juice and mix well. Stir in the chickpea flour. If the mixture is too dry and does not hold together, add a little water or olive oil or even some beaten egg to bind it. If it's too wet and sticky, add some more flour.

Take small spoonfuls of the mixture and, using your hands, mould them into balls. Roll them in sesame seeds and place them on the lined baking tray. Brush them lightly with olive oil.

Bake in the preheated oven for 20–25 minutes until golden brown and cooked right through. Serve hot with some pesto, warm pita bread triangles and a salad.

VARIATIONS
· Substitute coriander (cilantro) or basil for the parsley.
· Drizzle the cooked falafel with balsamic vinegar or glaze.
· Serve with a bowl of yoghurt, Tzatziki (see page 38) or Quick-and-easy Hummus (see page 33).
· Add a few drops of mushroom ketchup to boost the umami flavour.

FALAFEL SHAKSHUKA

//

Spicy shakshuka, a Middle Eastern speciality, is usually served for breakfast or brunch, but it's great to eat at any time of day. Along with the eggs we've added falafel, but vegans can enjoy this recipe without the eggs. You can make fresh falafel for this or use up some leftover ones.

SERVES 4
PREP 15 MINUTES
COOK 35–45 MINUTES

1 quantity cooked falafel of
   your choice
2 tbsp olive oil
1 red onion, diced
2 red (bell) peppers, deseeded
   and chopped
2 garlic cloves, crushed
1 red chilli, diced
1 tsp smoked paprika
1 tsp ground cumin
2 x 400g (14oz) tins (4 cups)
   chopped tomatoes
1 tbsp tomato purée
120ml (4fl oz/½ cup) passata
a pinch of sugar
a bunch of flat-leaf parsley,
   chopped
4 medium free-range eggs
Tahini Yoghurt Sauce (see page
   40), for drizzling
sea salt and freshly ground
   black pepper
crusty bread or flatbreads,
   to serve

Make and cook the falafel according to the instructions in the recipe.

Heat the oil in a large non-stick frying pan (skillet) over a medium heat. Add the onion, red peppers, garlic and chilli and cook, stirring occasionally, for 8–10 minutes until tender. Stir in the ground spices.

Add the tomatoes, tomato purée, passata and sugar and simmer for 15–20 minutes until the sauce starts to reduce and thicken. Season to taste with salt and pepper and stir in half the parsley.

Add the falafel and break in the eggs. Cover the pan and simmer gently for 10–15 minutes or until the falafel are warmed through and the eggs are cooked (whites are set, but yolks are still slightly runny). Sprinkle with the remaining parsley.

Drizzle with the Tahini Yoghurt Sauce and serve immediately with crusty bread or flatbreads to wipe up the spicy tomato sauce.

VARIATIONS
- Add a diced aubergine (eggplant).
- Add some chopped spinach or baby spinach leaves.
- Serve with Greek yoghurt swirled with pomegranate molasses.
- Use coriander (cilantro) instead of parsley.

CHILLI FALAFEL FRITTERS

//

In this recipe the chickpeas (garbanzo beans) are smashed with spices and herbs into a batter and fried into crisp golden fritters. You can serve them as a light lunch with salad or for brunch with crispy bacon and fried eggs.

SERVES 4
PREP 15 MINUTES
COOK 20 MINUTES

125g (4½oz/generous 1 cup) plain (all-purpose) flour
½ tsp baking powder
½ tsp sea salt
150ml (5fl oz/generous ½ cup) milk
1 medium free-range egg
400g (14oz) tin (1½ cups) chickpeas (garbanzo beans), rinsed and drained
a small bunch of spring onions (scallions), thinly sliced
1 red chilli, diced
1 tsp ground cumin
1 tsp ground coriander
grated zest of 1 lemon
a small bunch of flat-leaf parsley, chopped
olive or sunflower oil, for frying
freshly ground black pepper
Avocado Tahini Dip (see page 39), to serve

Sift the flour and baking powder into a mixing bowl. Add the salt and beat in the milk and egg, a little at a time, until you have a smooth, thick batter. Alternatively, use a food processor.

Add the chickpeas, squashing them with a spoon, and stir in the spring onions, chilli, ground spices, lemon zest and parsley. Season with black pepper.

Heat 2 tablespoons oil in a large non-stick frying pan (skillet) over a medium to high heat. Add large spoonfuls of the chickpea mixture, in batches. Don't overcrowd the pan – leave some space between the fritters. Cook for 3–4 minutes until golden brown and set underneath, then flip over and cook the other side. Remove and drain on kitchen paper (paper towels). Keep warm while you cook the rest of the mixture in the same way.

Serve the hot fritters with the Avocado Tahini Dip.

VARIATIONS
- Use chopped coriander (cilantro) or dill.
- Use dried chilli flakes instead of a fresh chilli.
- Serve with Tzatziki (see page 38) or a bowl of yoghurt swirled with harissa.
- Drizzle with chilli sauce.

SPICED PEA FALAFEL WITH ROASTED TOMATO SALAD

//

These crisply fried green falafel patties are delicious with a roasted tomato and creamy mozzarella or burrata salad. Serve the falafel with a bowl of yoghurt, or with one of the tahini sauces in the accompaniments chapter. You could even drizzle with pesto or pomegranate molasses.

SERVES 4
PREP 15 MINUTES
COOK 25 MINUTES

2 tsp cumin seeds
1 tsp coriander seeds
225g (8oz/1½ cups) frozen peas
2 x 400g (14oz) tins (3 cups) chickpeas (garbanzo beans), rinsed and drained
2 garlic cloves, crushed
1 onion, chopped
a bunch of coriander (cilantro), chopped
3–4 tbsp plain (all-purpose) flour
olive or vegetable oil, for shallow-frying
240g (8½oz/1 cup) Greek yoghurt
cayenne pepper, for dusting

ROASTED TOMATO SALAD
450g (1lb) cherry tomatoes on the vine
3 tbsp extra-virgin olive oil, plus extra for drizzling
100g (3½oz) rocket (arugula)
2 tbsp balsamic vinegar
250g (9oz) mozzarella or burrata, drained and sliced
sea salt and freshly ground black pepper

Preheat the oven to 200°C (180°C fan)/400°F/gas 6.

First, make the tomato salad: put the tomatoes in a roasting pan and drizzle with the olive oil. Season with salt and pepper and roast in the oven for 15 minutes, until softened and starting to blacken.

Meanwhile, toast the cumin and coriander seeds in a small frying pan (skillet) set over a medium to high heat, tossing occasionally, for 1–2 minutes or until they are fragrant and start to brown. Remove immediately before they burn and crush with a pestle and mortar.

Put the frozen peas in a bowl and pour some boiling water over them. Leave for 1 minute and then drain well. Pat the peas dry with kitchen paper (paper towels), as well as the chickpeas.

Blitz the peas and chickpeas in a food processor with the garlic, onion, most of the coriander and the crushed toasted seeds until they combine into a thick paste. Tip into a bowl and stir in the flour and some seasoning. If the mixture is too moist or not thick enough to roll into balls, add more flour. Take spoonfuls of the mixture and roll into balls (the size of golf balls). Flatten them slightly into patties.

Pour enough oil into a large non-stick frying pan (skillet) to cover the bottom and set over a medium heat. When it's hot, fry the patties, in batches, for 2 minutes each side or until crisp and golden.

Meanwhile, divide the roasted tomatoes on to four serving plates. Toss the rocket in the pan juices with the balsamic vinegar and add to the plate. Top with the mozzarella or burrata and drizzle with olive oil. Add the hot falafel and serve immediately with a bowl of yoghurt dusted with cayenne and sprinkled with the remaining coriander.

FALAFEL MEZE PLATTER

//

Serve this meze platter for four people as an informal light lunch, with pre-dinner drinks or as a first course, in which case it will serve six to eight. You can use any falafel, freshly made or reheated. It's important to serve everything really hot, especially the fried halloumi fingers.

SERVES 4
PREP 20 MINUTES
COOK 20–25 MINUTES

1 quantity cooked falafel of
　your choice

AUBERGINE (EGGPLANT) ROLLS
2 large aubergines (eggplants), cut
　lengthways into thin slices
olive oil, for brushing
150g (5½oz) feta cheese, crumbled
4 tbsp Greek yoghurt
1 tbsp green pesto
6 stoned (pitted) dates, diced
Greek thyme honey or pomegranate
　molasses, for drizzling
salt and freshly ground black pepper

HALLOUMI FINGERS
350g (12oz) halloumi cheese
4 tbsp plain (all-purpose) flour
2 tbsp za'atar
a good pinch of garlic powder
olive oil, for frying
1 tsp sumac

TO SERVE
olives, pickled chillies and warm pita
Hummus (see page 33)
Tzatziki (see page 38)
Tahini Yoghurt Sauce (see page 40)

Make and cook the falafel according to the instructions in the recipe.

Make the aubergine rolls: brush the aubergine slices with oil and season with salt and pepper. Heat a large ridged griddle pan over a medium to high heat and cook the aubergine, a few slices at a time, for 2–3 minutes each side until golden brown. Drain on kitchen paper (paper towels).

In a bowl, mix together the feta, yoghurt, pesto and dates. Thinly spread a little mixture over the griddled aubergine slices and roll up from the thin end. Place seam-side down on a serving plate and drizzle with honey or pomegranate molasses.

Cut the halloumi into 12 fat 'fingers' and dust lightly with a mixture of the flour, za'atar and garlic powder. Heat enough oil to cover the bottom of a non-stick frying pan (skillet) and set over a medium to high heat. Fry the halloumi, in batches, for 1–2 minutes each side, or until crisp and golden brown. Remove and drain on kitchen paper. Transfer to a serving plate and dust lightly with sumac.

Put the hot falafel on another serving plate. Add some bowls of olives, pickled chillies, Hummus, Tzatziki and Tahini Yoghurt Sauce for people to help themselves. Serve immediately with warm pita bread, cut into triangles, to mop up the sauces and dips.

VARIATIONS
- Use courgettes (zucchini) instead of aubergines.
- Serve with Baba Ghanoush (see page 79) or Skordalia (see page 34).
- Serve with yoghurt swirled with harissa or chilli sauce.
- Add some crusty bread or seedy crackers.

THAI GREEN CURRY FALAFEL BURGERS

Who would have thought that falafel could be so versatile? We've added Thai flavourings and some green curry paste to create really spicy burgers. However, you could mould the mixture into small balls and shallow-fry them in the same way to serve with satay sauce instead. Vegans can use a vegan-friendly nam pla or soy sauce.

SERVES 4
PREP 20 MINUTES
CHILL 30 MINUTES
COOK 8–10 MINUTES

2 x 400g (14oz) tins (3 cups) chickpeas (garbanzo beans), rinsed and drained
4 garlic cloves, crushed
2 lemongrass stalks, peeled and diced
6 spring onions (scallions), chopped
1 bunch of coriander (cilantro), chopped
1 red bird's-eye chilli, diced
5 kaffir lime leaves, thinly sliced
2 tbsp Thai green curry paste
2 tsp nam pla (Thai fish sauce)
3 tbsp chickpea (gram) flour, plus extra for dusting
groundnut (peanut) oil, for frying
4 burger buns, split and toasted
shredded lettuce and sliced tomato, to serve
sweet chilli sauce, for drizzling

Blitz the chickpeas in a food processor with the garlic, lemongrass, spring onions, coriander, chilli, lime leaves, curry paste and nam pla until you have a thick paste.

Tip into a bowl and stir in the flour. If the mixture is too moist or not thick enough to form into burgers, add more flour, so it holds its shape together.

Divide into four equal-sized portions and, using your hands, mould each one into a burger shape, flattening it slightly. Place the burgers on a plate, cover and chill in the fridge for 30 minutes to firm up. Dust lightly with flour just before cooking.

Pour enough oil into a large non-stick frying pan (skillet) to cover the bottom and set over a medium heat. When it's hot, fry the burgers for 4–5 minutes each side or until crisp and golden brown.

Fill the burger buns with some lettuce, tomatoes and the burgers. Drizzle with sweet chilli sauce and serve.

VARIATIONS
• Serve the burgers (without the buns) with some boiled rice and salad.
• Use red Thai curry paste.
• Add some fresh root ginger, galangal or turmeric.

CHEESY FALAFEL QUESADILLAS

//

For these delicious quesadillas oozing with melted cheese we've used a spiced mashed chickpea (garbanzo bean) mixture, which you can prepare in minutes. Eat them as a snack, for brunch or as a light lunch with some salad.

SERVES 4
PREP 15 MINUTES
COOK 20 MINUTES

2 x 400g (14oz) tins (3 cups) chickpeas (garbanzo beans), rinsed and drained
1 tsp ground cumin
½ tsp dried chilli flakes
4 spring onions (scallions), thinly sliced
a handful of coriander (cilantro), finely chopped
150g (5½oz/1½ cups) grated Cheddar or Monterey Jack cheese
6 large flour tortillas
2 tbsp vegetable or olive oil
sea salt and freshly ground black pepper
guacamole, salsa and soured cream, to serve

Dry the chickpeas with kitchen paper (paper towels) and place in a bowl with the cumin, chilli and a little salt and pepper. Mash coarsely with a potato masher.

Add the spring onions, coriander and grated cheese and mix well.

Spread one-third of the mixture over a flour tortilla, but not quite up to the edge – leave a small border. Cover with another tortilla, pressing down firmly around the edge. Repeat with the remaining filling and tortillas.

Heat the oil in a large non-stick frying pan (skillet) over a low to medium heat. Carefully slide a quesadilla into the hot pan and cook for 3–4 minutes until golden brown underneath. Turn it over and cook the other side for 3–4 minutes until crisp, golden and the cheese is melting. Remove from the pan and cook the remaining quesadillas in the same way.

Serve the quesadillas, cut into wedges, with some guacamole, salsa and soured cream.

VARIATIONS
- Add a dash of lime juice to the filling or serve with lime wedges.
- Add 1 teaspoon chipotle paste or a diced fresh chilli.
- Add some cooked chopped spinach.
- Add diced tomato, (bell) peppers or sweetcorn.

SALADS

WARM FALAFEL SALAD WITH ROASTED CARROTS

//

You can make fresh falafel for this colourful salad or heat up some leftover ones in the oven or microwave. Vegans can use dairy-free yoghurt.

SERVES 4
PREP 15 MINUTES
COOK 30–40 MINUTES

1 quantity cooked falafel of
    your choice
500g (1lb 2oz) baby carrots,
    trimmed
1 red onion, cut into wedges
1 tsp smoked paprika
1 tsp ground cumin
1 tsp crushed coriander seeds
3 tbsp fruity extra-virgin olive oil
75g (2½oz/½ cup) stoned (pitted)
    dates, cut into thin slivers
a bunch of coriander (cilantro),
    finely chopped
a handful of mint, finely chopped
grated zest and juice of 1 orange
seeds of ½ pomegranate
pomegranate molasses, for
    drizzling
120ml (4fl oz/½ cup) Greek
    yoghurt
sea salt and freshly ground
    black pepper
warm pita breads or flatbreads,
    to serve

Make and cook the falafel according to the instructions in the recipe.

Preheat the oven to 180°C (160°C fan)/350°F/gas 4.

Put the carrots, onion, ground spices, coriander seeds and olive oil in a bowl and stir until well coated with oil. Tip into a baking dish and roast in the preheated oven for 30–40 minutes, or until the carrots and onion are tender.

Transfer to a serving dish and stir in the dates, most of the herbs, and orange zest and juice. Season to taste with salt and pepper. Arrange the hot falafel on top and sprinkle with the remaining herbs and pomegranate seeds.

Swirl the pomegranate molasses into the yoghurt and serve on the side for people to help themselves. Eat warm with toasted pita or flatbreads.

VARIATIONS
- Use a lemon instead of an orange.
- Sprinkle with crumbled feta or goat's cheese.
- For a more substantial salad, mix the roasted carrots and onions into some couscous or quinoa.
- Use flat-leaf parsley.
- Add some sumac for a lemony flavour.

ROASTED AUBERGINE AND FALAFEL SALAD

//

This salad is best eaten warm, but you can put any leftovers in a sealed container and eat it cold for lunch the following day. Falafel made with peas, pumpkin, squash or sweet potatoes are delicious with this.

SERVES 4
PREP 20 MINUTES
COOK 20 MINUTES

1 quantity cooked falafel of
   your choice
2 aubergines (eggplants),
   chopped into 2.5cm (1in) cubes
3 tbsp fruity extra-virgin olive oil,
   plus extra for griddling
1 radicchio, trimmed and
   separated into leaves
balsamic vinegar, for drizzling
1 small red onion, diced
75g (2½oz) baby spinach leaves
dukkah or toasted seeds,
   for sprinkling
harissa, to serve

**YOGHURT AND TAHINI
DRESSING**

1 garlic clove, crushed
a handful of parsley or coriander
   (cilantro), finely chopped
2 tbsp tahini
2 tbsp olive oil
grated zest and juice of ½ lemon
1 tsp clear honey
240ml (8fl oz/1 cup) natural
   yoghurt
sea salt and freshly ground
   black pepper

Make and cook the falafel according to the instructions in the recipe.

Preheat the oven to 190°C (170°C fan)/375°F/gas 5.

Make the dressing: blitz the garlic and herbs in a blender. Add the tahini, olive oil, lemon zest and juice and honey and blitz until well combined. Spoon into a bowl and stir in the yoghurt. Season to taste with salt and pepper.

Toss the aubergines in the olive oil and arrange them on a baking tray (cookie sheet). Cook in the preheated oven for 20 minutes, turning halfway through, until golden brown and tender.

Meanwhile, lightly oil a griddle pan and set over a high heat. Cook the radicchio for 2–3 minutes until slightly charred on both sides. Remove and drizzle with balsamic vinegar.

Put the roasted aubergines, radicchio, red onion and spinach in a large bowl. Lightly toss everything together and top with the hot falafel. Drizzle with the yoghurt and tahini dressing and sprinkle with dukkah or toasted seeds. Serve warm with some harissa on the side.

VARIATIONS
· Top with fresh pomegranate seeds.
· Use red chicory instead of radicchio.
· Toss the salad in a lemony vinaigrette dressing.
· Make with roasted red and yellow (bell) peppers.

GREEK FALAFEL AND HORIATIKI VILLAGE SALAD

In Greece, falafel are known as *revithokeftedes* and they are usually made with boiled, not soaked, chickpeas (garbanzo beans). We suggest that you use the little feta-stuffed falafel bites in the wraps, sandwiches and snacks chapter, but any sort will work well. Don't worry if you have any leftover tahini sauce – it will keep in the fridge in a sealed container for up to 3 days.

SERVES 4
PREP 20 MINUTES

1 quantity cooked Greek Spinach and Feta Falafel Bites (see page 96)
400g (14oz) tomatoes on the vine, quartered
½ cucumber, thickly sliced and quartered
1 green (bell) pepper, deseeded and cut into chunks
½ red onion, very thinly sliced
12 black olives, e.g. Kalamata
2 tsp capers
150g (5½oz) feta cheese, cubed
½ tsp dried oregano
fruity extra-virgin olive oil, for drizzling
red wine vinegar, for drizzling
freshly ground black pepper
crusty bread, to serve

TAHINI SAUCE
2 garlic cloves
½ tsp sea salt
100g (3½oz/⅓ cup) tahini
120ml (4fl oz/½ cup) lemon juice
3–4 tbsp cold water

Make and cook the falafel according to the instructions in the recipe.

Make the tahini sauce: crush the garlic and salt in a pestle and mortar. Blitz in a blender with the tahini and lemon juice, adding enough water to thin it to a sauce. Pour into a jug and set aside while you make the salad.

Mix together the tomatoes, cucumber, green pepper, red onion, olives and capers in a bowl. Scatter the feta over the top and sprinkle with oregano. Season to taste with black pepper and drizzle with olive oil and red wine vinegar.

Divide the salad among four serving plates and add the falafel (hot or cold). Drizzle the falafel with the tahini sauce and serve with crusty bread.

VARIATIONS
· Use red or yellow (bell) peppers.
· Use the small, ridged Greek cucumbers.
· Add some pickled chillies.
· Blitz the tahini sauce with a handful of flat-leaf parsley.

LEBANESE FALAFEL AND FATTOUSH SALAD

To make the best crunchy fattoush salad, you need really fresh good-quality vegetables and herbs. Use the best sweet, ripe and juicy tomatoes you can find. This is also a great way of using up stale pita bread. You can use freshly cooked hot falafel or reheat some leftover ones – even cold falafel are delicious. Vegans can use dairy-free yoghurt in the sauce.

SERVES 4
PREP 15 MINUTES
COOK 3–4 MINUTES

1 quantity cooked falafel of
    your choice
400g (14oz) ripe tomatoes,
    chopped
1 red onion, diced
1 green (bell) pepper, deseeded
    and diced
½ cucumber, chopped
a bunch of radishes, trimmed
    and thinly sliced
1 cos (romaine) lettuce, shredded
a bunch of mint, chopped
a bunch of flat-leaf parsley,
    chopped
4 pita breads
2 tbsp olive oil
Tahini Yoghurt Sauce (see page
    40), for drizzling

LEMON DRESSING

grated zest and juice of 1 lemon
5 tbsp extra-virgin olive oil
1 garlic clove, crushed
1 tbsp sumac
¼ tsp ground cinnamon
sea salt and freshly ground
    black pepper

Make and cook the falafel according to the instructions in the recipe.

Put the tomatoes, red onion, green pepper, cucumber, radishes and lettuce in a large serving bowl and mix together with the chopped herbs.

Make the lemon dressing: whisk all the ingredients together in a bowl or shake vigorously in a screw-top jar.

Lightly toast the pita breads and break them roughly into small pieces. Fry them in the oil in a non-stick frying pan (skillet) set over a medium heat for 3–4 minutes or until browned and crispy. Remove and drain on kitchen paper (paper towels), then add them to the salad.

Gently toss the salad in the lemon dressing and divide among four serving plates. Top with the falafel (hot or cold) and drizzle with Tahini Yoghurt Sauce. Serve immediately while the pita is still crisp.

VARIATIONS
- Use thinly sliced spring onions (scallions).
- Drizzle with Lemony Green Tahini Sauce (see page 41).
- Serve with intensely garlic Skordalia (see page 34).
- Vary the herbs: try basil, mint or coriander (cilantro).
- Add some za'atar or a squeeze of pomegranate molasses to the dressing.

FALAFEL TABBOULEH SALAD

///

Nutty-tasting bulgur wheat gives this tabbouleh salad some delicious crunch. You can use any falafel, freshly cooked or cold or reheated leftovers. For a light meal, serve it with a crisp salad. Vegans can use dairy-free yoghurt.

SERVES 4
PREP 15 MINUTES
COOK 10 MINUTES

1 quantity cooked falafel of
    your choice
200g (7oz/scant 1¼ cups) bulgur
    wheat (dried weight)
240ml (8fl oz/1 cup) vegetable
    stock
30g (1oz/generous ¼ cup)
    pine nuts
a bunch of spring onions
    (scallions), finely chopped
225g (8oz) ripe baby plum
    tomatoes, diced
a bunch of flat-leaf parsley,
    finely chopped
a handful of mint, finely chopped
juice of 2 lemons
3 tbsp fruity extra-virgin olive oil
sea salt and freshly ground
    black pepper

LEMON YOGHURT DRIZZLE
120g (4oz/½ cup) natural yoghurt
grated zest and juice of ½ lemon

Make and cook the falafel according to the instructions in the recipe.

Put the bulgur wheat and stock in a saucepan and bring to the boil. Reduce the heat, cover and simmer for 5 minutes. Take the pan off the heat and leave in the covered pan to continue cooking for at least another 5 minutes, or until the grains of bulgur wheat are tender and have absorbed most or all of the stock.

Meanwhile, set a dry non-stick frying pan (skillet) over a medium heat and, when it's hot, add the pine nuts. Toast for 1–2 minutes, stirring often, until they start to turn golden brown – don't let them burn. Remove immediately.

Tip the warm bulgur wheat into a bowl and stir in the spring onions, tomatoes, herbs, lemon juice and olive oil. Season to taste with salt and pepper.

Make the lemon yoghurt drizzle: mix the yoghurt with the lemon zest and juice.

Divide the bulgur wheat tabbouleh among four serving plates and top with the falafel (hot or cold). Sprinkle with the toasted pine nuts and serve, drizzled with lemon yoghurt.

VARIATIONS
· Sprinkle with pomegranate seeds.
· Add some diced feta or griddled halloumi.
· Add some basil, coriander (cilantro), baby spinach or
    shredded kale.
· Add roasted (bell) peppers, red onions and baby carrots.

FALAFEL MEZE SALAD BOWL

///

A meze salad bowl is a movable feast and you can add practically anything – see the suggestions at the end of the recipe. Any freshly cooked or reheated falafel work well. You can buy pouches of mixed cooked grains, so why not use one of these for convenience if you're in a hurry?

SERVES 4
PREP 15 MINUTES

1 quantity cooked falafel of
    your choice
100g (3½oz) baby spinach, rocket
    (arugula) or shredded cos
    (romaine) lettuce
2 tbsp fruity extra-virgin olive oil,
    plus extra for drizzling
juice of ½ lemon
150g (5½oz) feta cheese, cubed
4 bottled roasted red and yellow
    (bell) peppers, sliced
4 pickled Lebanese chillies
500g (1lb 2oz) cooked grains, e.g.
    brown rice, quinoa, freekeh
120g (4oz/½ cup) Tzatziki (see
    page 38)
a handful of chopped parsley
a handful of chopped coriander
    (cilantro)
sea salt and freshly ground
    black pepper
warm pita breads, to serve

Make and cook the falafel according to the instructions in the recipe.

Toss the spinach, rocket or lettuce leaves in the olive oil and lemon juice. Season to taste with salt and pepper.

Divide them among four shallow serving bowls and top with the feta, red and yellow peppers and pickled chillies.

Add the cooked grains, a few spoonfuls of tzatziki and the hot falafel. Sprinkle with the parsley or coriander and serve with warm toasted pita breads, cut into triangles.

VARIATIONS
- Add Quick-and-easy Hummus (see page 33) or Baba Ghanoush (see page 79).
- Add some drained tinned chickpeas (garbanzo beans) or Greek gigantes beans.
- Fry or griddle sliced halloumi and use instead of feta.
- Put a slice of feta on top of the salad leaves and sprinkle with dried oregano and olive oil.
- Add some bottled artichoke hearts, stuffed vine leaves, black or green olives and sun-blush tomatoes.

PUMPKIN OR SQUASH FALAFEL BUDDHA BOWLS

///

These healthy Buddha bowls are packed with nutritional goodness and flavour. We've used sweet-tasting pumpkin or squash falafel, which complement the bulgur wheat and roasted vegetables, but you can use traditional or flavoured falafel as long as they are hot (freshly made or reheated).

SERVES 4
PREP 20 MINUTES
COOK 30–35 MINUTES

1 quantity cooked Pumpkin or
    Squash Falafel (see page 23)
1 large red onion, cut into wedges
2 red or yellow (bell) peppers,
    deseeded and cut into chunks
225g (8oz) cherry tomatoes
3 garlic cloves, unpeeled
a few sprigs of thyme
3 sprigs of rosemary
3 tbsp olive oil
200g (7oz) kale, trimmed and
    large stems removed
a handful of flat-leaf parsley,
    chopped
200g (7oz/scant 1¼ cups) bulgur
    wheat (dried weight)
240ml (8fl oz/1 cup) vegetable
    stock
1 ripe avocado, peeled, stoned
    (pitted) and thinly sliced
a handful of baby spinach or
    rocket (arugula)
balsamic vinegar, for drizzling
sea salt and freshly ground
    black pepper

Make and cook the falafel according to the instructions in the recipe.

Preheat the oven to 200°C (180°C fan)/400°F/gas 6.

Meanwhile, put the red onion, pepper and tomatoes in a large roasting pan. Tuck the garlic down between the vegetables and sprinkle with herbs. Drizzle with olive oil and season with salt and pepper.

Roast in the preheated oven for 25–30 minutes or until the vegetables are tender. Add the kale to the pan, stirring it into the roasted vegetables, and return to the oven for 5 minutes. Squeeze the garlic out of their skins and stir into the vegetables with the parsley.

While the vegetables are roasting, put the bulgur wheat and stock in a saucepan and bring to the boil. Reduce the heat, cover and simmer for 5 minutes. Take the pan off the heat and leave in the covered pan to continue cooking for at least another 5 minutes, or until the grains of bulgur wheat are tender and have absorbed most or all of the stock.

Divide the roasted vegetables, avocado, spinach or rocket and the warm bulgur wheat into four shallow serving bowls. Top with the hot falafel and drizzle with balsamic vinegar.

VARIATIONS
· Stir in cooked broccoli or roasted cauliflower.
· Substitute couscous, quinoa or brown rice for the
  bulgur wheat.
· Add toasted pine nuts or sesame seeds.
· Drizzle with Tahini Yoghurt Sauce (see page 40).
· Add a spoonful of Tzatziki (see page 38) or Quick-and-
  easy Hummus (see page 33).

SWEET POTATO FALAFEL WITH CRUNCHY FENNEL SALAD

A fresh spicy green chutney is a good accompaniment to falafel. This one needs no cooking and can be made in a blender in minutes. You can also swirl it into a bowl of yoghurt to serve on the side. You can use any hot falafel (freshly made or reheated).

SERVES 4
PREP 25 MINUTES

1 quantity cooked Sweet Potato
    Falafel (see page 28)
1 large or 2 small fennel bulbs
    with green feathery fronds
2 juicy oranges
1 ripe avocado, peeled, stoned
    (pitted) and cubed
12 black olives, stoned (pitted)
seeds of ½ pomegranate
extra-virgin olive oil, for drizzling
sea salt crystals

SPICY HERB CHUTNEY

a bunch of coriander (cilantro),
    finely chopped
a handful of mint, finely chopped
2 spring onions (scallions),
    chopped
1 garlic clove, crushed
1 tbsp diced fresh root ginger
1 green chilli, diced
1 tbsp peanuts
1 tsp sugar
juice of ½ lemon
2 tbsp olive oil

Make and cook the falafel according to the instructions in the recipe.

Make the spicy herb chutney: put all the ingredients in a blender and blitz to a bright green purée. Transfer to a bowl. If it's too thick for drizzling, stir in a little water.

Trim the fennel base and tops. Cut off the feathery fronds and set aside. Thinly slice the fennel bulbs and place in a bowl.

With a sharp knife, cut off and discard all the peel and white pith from the oranges. Cut the oranges horizontally into slices and add to the fennel together with any leftover juice. Add the avocado and black olives and mix together gently.

Finely chop the green feathery fennel and sprinkle over the salad with the pomegranate seeds. Drizzle plenty of olive oil over the top and sprinkle with salt.

Divide the fennel salad among four serving plates. Add the hot falafel and drizzle the chutney over the falafel. Serve immediately.

VARIATIONS
- Use basil or flat-leaf parsley in the chutney.
- Substitute a spoonful of peanut butter for the peanuts.
- Add some toasted fennel seeds or dried chilli flakes to the salad.

SPINACH FALAFEL WITH CRUNCHY BEAN AND BACON SALAD

//

A crunchy bean salad perfectly complements spinach falafel. If you're vegetarian or vegan, just leave out the bacon. As always, you can use any falafel in this dish, freshly made or reheated.

SERVES 4
PREP 15 MINUTES
COOK 7–8 MINUTES

1 quantity cooked Spinach and Chilli Falafel (see page 24)
200g (7oz) fine green beans, trimmed and halved
8 thin rashers (slices) streaky bacon
400g (14oz) tin (2 cups) cannellini beans, rinsed and drained
1 garlic clove, crushed
a large handful of flat-leaf parsley, finely chopped
2 tbsp capers, roughly chopped
¼ tsp dried chilli flakes
4 tbsp extra-virgin olive oil
grated zest and juice of ½ lemon
Tahini Yoghurt Sauce (see page 40), for drizzling
sea salt and freshly ground black pepper

Make and cook the falafel according to the instructions in the recipe.

Bring a pan of water to the boil and add the green beans. Boil for 2 minutes, or until they are just tender but still crisp. Drain and plunge them into a bowl of iced water to cool them. Remove and pat dry with kitchen paper (paper towels).

Cook the bacon under a hot grill (broiler) or in a non-stick frying pan (skillet) until golden brown and crispy.

Put the green beans in a bowl with the tinned beans, garlic, parsley, capers, chilli flakes, olive oil, lemon zest and juice. Toss everything gently and then season to taste with salt and pepper. Crumble the bacon over the top.

Serve the hot falafel, drizzled with Tahini Yoghurt Sauce, with the bean salad.

Tip: If you're not using freshly made falafel, don't reheat the cold falafel in a microwave as they will be soft and mushy. Instead, reheat them in a preheated oven at 180°C (160°C fan)/350°F/gas 4 for 15 minutes until heated through. Alternatively, shallow-fry them in oil over medium heat for about 4–5 minutes.

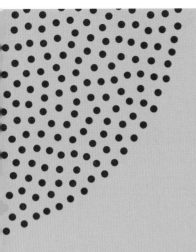

MAIN MEALS

FALAFEL AND GARLIC CHICKEN SAUTÉ

//

Instead of serving the hummus on the side, it's swirled around the plate to make a delicious edible border for the garlicky chicken and hot falafel. You can use any flavoured falafel, freshly made or reheated.

SERVES 4
PREP 20 MINUTES
COOK 10–15 MINUTES

1 quantity cooked falafel of
    your choice
4 tbsp olive oil
450g (1lb) skinned chicken
    breast fillets
4 garlic cloves, crushed
¼ teaspoon sweet paprika
juice of 1 small lemon
a handful of flat-leaf parsley,
    chopped
1 quantity Quick-and-easy
    Hummus (see page 33)
a handful of rocket (arugula) or
    baby spinach leaves
seeds of ½ pomegranate
sea salt and freshly ground
    black pepper
cooked rice, quinoa or couscous,
    to serve

Make and cook the falafel according to the instructions in the recipe.

Heat the olive oil in a large non-stick frying pan (skillet) over a medium heat and cook the chicken for 10–15 minutes, turning halfway through, until it's golden brown on the outside and cooked right through.

Add the garlic towards the end to prevent it browning. Season with salt and pepper and dust with paprika. Stir in the lemon juice and parsley.

Smear the hummus around the edge of four serving plates and arrange the garlicky chicken, hot falafel and rocket or spinach in the centre. Sprinkle the pomegranate seeds over the top and serve with rice, quinoa or couscous.

VARIATIONS
· Use griddled lean lamb instead of chicken.
· Serve with roasted vegetables.
· Instead of salad leaves, use cooked spinach.
· Substitute mint or coriander (cilantro) for the parsley.
· Drizzle with pomegranate molasses or hot sauce.

SPAGHETTI NAPOLETANA WITH FALAFEL

We've added falafel instead of meatballs to a classic tomato sauce to serve with pasta. It works so well you'll be amazed you've never tried it before. It's a great idea for using up leftover falafel. Vegans can use vegan-friendly cheese.

SERVES 4
PREP 10 MINUTES
COOK 25 MINUTES

1 quantity cooked Traditional Falafel (see page 14)
500g (1lb 2oz) spaghetti (dried weight)
olive oil, for tossing
grated Parmesan, to serve

NAPOLETANA SAUCE
3 tbsp olive oil
2 onions, finely chopped
3 garlic cloves, crushed
400g (14oz) tin (scant 2 cups) chopped tomatoes
450g (1lb) ripe tomatoes, roughly chopped
1 tbsp tomato purée
a pinch of sugar
a small handful of basil leaves, torn
a splash of balsamic vinegar
sea salt and freshly ground black pepper

Make and cook the falafel according to the instructions in the recipe.

Make the napoletana sauce: heat the oil in a large non-stick frying pan (skillet) over a low to medium heat and cook the onion and garlic, stirring occasionally, for 8–10 minutes until tender but not browned.

Stir in the tomatoes, tomato purée and sugar and increase the heat to medium. Cook for about 10 minutes, or until the sauce thickens and reduces. Season to taste with salt and pepper, and add the basil and balsamic vinegar.

Reduce the heat and add the cooked falafel to the sauce. Simmer very gently for 5 minutes or so until they are heated right through.

Meanwhile, cook the spaghetti in a large pan of boiling salted water (following the instructions on the packet) until just tender but still al dente. Drain well and return to the pan. Toss in a little olive oil.

Divide the spaghetti among four serving plates and top with the falafel and napoletana sauce. Serve immediately, sprinkled with grated Parmesan.

VARIATIONS
· Use any pasta, especially linguine or tagliatelle.
· Sprinkle with torn basil or chopped parsley.
· Use two tins of chopped tomatoes if you don't have fresh ones.
· Add a diced chilli to the sauce.

FALAFEL, SPINACH AND PASTA BAKE

//

A healthy, filling pasta bake makes a quick-and-easy supper dish. In this veggie version, we've substituted falafel for the usual meatballs and added some harissa and Middle Eastern spice. Vegans can use vegan-friendly grated cheese.

SERVES 4
PREP 15 MINUTES
COOK 35–40 MINUTES

1 quantity cooked falafel of
    your choice
250g (9oz) pasta shapes, e.g.
    fusilli, rigatoni, penne (dried
    weight)
2 tbsp olive oil
1 red onion, diced
1 red (bell) pepper, deseeded
    and diced
1 yellow (bell) pepper, deseeded
    and diced
½ tsp ground cumin
1 tbsp harissa paste
400g (14oz) tin (scant 2 cups)
    cherry tomatoes
240ml (8fl oz/1 cup) passata
1 tbsp tomato purée
1 tsp dried basil or oregano
100g (3½oz) baby spinach leaves
50g (2oz/½ cup) grated cheese,
    e.g. halloumi or Parmesan
sea salt and freshly ground
    black pepper
chopped parsley, to serve

Make and cook the falafel according to the instructions in the recipe.

Preheat the oven to 200°C (180°C fan)/400°F/gas 6.

Cook the pasta in a large pan of boiling salted water (following the instructions on the packet) until just tender but still al dente. Drain well.

Meanwhile, heat the oil in a large non-stick frying pan (skillet) over a low heat and cook the onion, stirring occasionally, for 8–10 minutes, or until softened. Add the peppers and cook for 5 minutes. Stir in the cumin and harissa. Increase the heat to medium and add the tomatoes, passata, tomato purée and herbs. Cook for 5–10 minutes until the mixture begins to reduce and thicken slightly. Stir in the spinach and season to taste with salt and pepper.

Put the cooked pasta and falafel into a large shallow baking dish. Pour over the tomato sauce mixture and sprinkle the grated cheese over the top.

Bake in the preheated oven for 15 minutes or until the sauce is bubbling and the top is crisp and golden brown. Sprinkle with parsley and serve immediately.

VARIATIONS
- Crumble some feta over the top before baking in the oven.
- Use defrosted frozen spinach instead of baby leaf.
- Add some ground coriander and cinnamon.
- Add some cubed aubergine (eggplant), chopped prunes or dried apricots.

MOROCCAN SPICED FALAFEL AND VEGETABLE TAGINE

//

Adding falafel to a warming tagine makes it more substantial. Vegans can use dairy-free yoghurt and agave nectar instead of honey.

SERVES 4
PREP 20 MINUTES
COOK 35 MINUTES

1 quantity cooked falafel of choice
2 tbsp olive oil
1 red onion, thinly sliced
3 garlic cloves, crushed
1 small aubergine (eggplant), cubed
2 tsp grated fresh root ginger
1 tsp cumin seeds
1 tsp ground coriander
1 tsp ground cinnamon
½ tsp ground turmeric
1 tbsp harissa, plus extra to serve
400g (14oz) tin (1½ cups)
    chickpeas (garbanzo beans),
    rinsed and drained
3 carrots, sliced
1 small butternut squash, peeled
    and cubed
400g (14oz) tomatoes, diced
125g (2oz/¾ cup) stoned dates
300ml (2fl oz/1¼ cups) vegetable
    stock
1 tsp clear honey
1 preserved lemon, rinsed, skin
    only, thinly sliced
a bunch of flat-leaf parsley,
    chopped
sea salt and black pepper
couscous, to serve
Greek yoghurt, to serve

Make and cook the falafel according to the instructions in the recipe.

Heat the olive oil in a large saucepan over a low to medium heat, and cook the onion, garlic and aubergine, stirring occasionally, for about 8 minutes until tender and golden. Stir in the ginger, seeds, ground spices and harissa and cook for 1 minute.

Stir in the chickpeas, carrot, squash, tomatoes and dates. Add the stock and bring to the boil. Reduce the heat, cover the pan and simmer gently for 10 minutes, then add the falafel. Cook for a further 10–15 minutes until the vegetables are tender and the liquid has reduced and thickened.

Season to taste with salt and pepper, and stir in the honey together with the preserved lemon and parsley.

Serve immediately on a bed of hot couscous with a bowl of yoghurt, swirled with harissa, on the side.

VARIATIONS
· Use prunes or dried apricots instead of dates.
· Add some cauliflower florets, parsnips or pumpkin.
· Use mint or coriander (cilantro) instead of parsley.
· Swirl some tahini or pomegranate molasses into the Greek yoghurt.
· Sprinkle with toasted flaked almonds.

SPINACH FALAFEL SKEWERS WITH SPANAKORIZO

You will need to use a firm falafel mixture made with soaked dried chickpeas (garbanzo beans) for the kebabs, so they don't fall apart. Chilling them before cooking will also help to firm them up. Spanakorizo is a traditional Greek pilaf made with spinach, dill and fresh lemon.

SERVES 4
PREP 25 MINUTES
COOK 30 MINUTES

1 quantity uncooked falafel
    mixture (made with
    soaked dried chickpeas/
    garbanzo beans)
2 red onions, peeled and
    quartered
2 yellow (bell) peppers, deseeded
    and cut into chunks
350g (12oz) button mushrooms
olive oil, for brushing
Tahini Yoghurt Sauce (see page
    40), for drizzling

SPANAKORIZO
4 tbsp fruity extra-virgin olive oil
1 onion, diced
4 spring onions (scallions), thinly
    sliced
2 garlic cloves, crushed
1kg (2lb 4oz) spinach, washed,
    trimmed and coarsely shredded
175g (6oz/generous ¾ cup)
    long-grain rice (dried weight)
a small bunch of dill, chopped
350ml (12fl oz/1½ cups) hot
    vegetable stock
juice of 1 lemon
sea salt and black pepper

Make the spanakorizo: heat the olive oil in a large saucepan over a low heat. Cook the onion, spring onions and garlic, stirring occasionally, for 10 minutes until softened. Stir in the spinach and mix well. Cook for 1 minute until the spinach wilts and reduces in bulk.

Stir in the rice, dill and some seasoning. Add the hot stock and bring to the boil. Reduce the heat, cover the pan and simmer gently for about 15 minutes, or until the rice is cooked and tender and the liquid has been absorbed. Add the lemon juice and fluff up with a fork. Leave covered until you're ready to serve.

Meanwhile, take large spoonfuls of the falafel mixture and shape into balls. Thread them onto soaked wooden skewers, alternating with the onions, peppers and mushrooms. Brush lightly with olive oil and season with salt and pepper.

Place the kebabs in a foil-lined grill pan and cook under a preheated hot grill (broiler) for about 10 minutes, turning occasionally, until the vegetables are tender and slightly charred and the falafel are cooked and browned. Alternatively, lay them in an oiled large griddle pan and cook, turning, for 8–10 minutes.

Serve the kebabs with the warm spanakorizo and some Tahini Yoghurt Sauce for drizzling.

VARIATIONS
· Add cherry tomatoes, courgette (zucchini) or aubergine (eggplant) to the kebabs.
· Use leek instead of onion in the spanakorizo.

FALAFEL HASH MEZE WITH BABA GHANOUSH

You can make the baba ghanoush in advance and keep it covered in the fridge until you're ready to cook the hash. We've used tinned chickpeas (garbanzo beans), but it's also a delicious way to use up leftover cooked falafel. Just add them to the pan, warm through and mash coarsely.

SERVES 4
PREP 20 MINUTES
DRAIN 30 MINUTES
COOK 25 MINUTES

3 tbsp olive oil
1 red onion, chopped
2 garlic cloves, crushed
1 tsp ground cumin
1 tsp ground coriander
2 x 400g (14oz) tins (3 cups)
    chickpeas (garbanzo beans),
    rinsed and drained
12 baby plum tomatoes,
    quartered
juice of 1 lemon
a handful of coriander (cilantro),
    finely chopped
salad and warm pita breads,
    to serve

BABA GHANOUSH
2 large aubergines (eggplants)
2 garlic cloves, crushed
juice of 1 lemon
2 tbsp olive oil, plus extra for
    drizzling
a few sprigs of flat-leaf parsley,
    chopped
pomegranate seeds, for sprinkling
sea salt and freshly ground
    black pepper

Make the baba ghanoush: using tongs, hold the aubergines over a gas flame until really charred and so soft that they lose their shape and start to collapse. Alternatively, char them under a hot grill (broiler). Leave to cool.

Cut the aubergines in half and scoop out the soft flesh into a sieve. Leave for 30 minutes to drain away any excess liquid. Transfer to a bowl and mash the aubergine with a fork. Stir in the garlic, lemon juice, olive oil and parsley. Season with salt and pepper and sprinkle with pomegranate seeds.

Heat the olive oil in a large non-stick frying pan (skillet) over a medium heat. Cook the onion and garlic, stirring occasionally, for 6–8 minutes until softened. Stir in the spices and cook for 1 minute. Add the chickpeas and heat through, then mash coarsely in the pan with a potato masher. Stir in the tomatoes and continue cooking for 2 minutes. Add the lemon juice, coriander and season to taste.

Divide among four serving plates and serve immediately with salad and some warm pita breads. Let people help themselves to the baba ghanoush.

VARIATIONS
- Serve with feta or griddled halloumi.
- Use flat-leaf parsley instead of coriander (cilantro).
- Add 1 tablespoon red wine vinegar to the baba ghanoush.
- For a thicker version, stir in 1 tablespoon fresh breadcrumbs.
- Add some dried chilli flakes to the hash or drizzle with chilli sauce.

FALAFEL PAD THAI

//

If you've never thought of adding falafel to a pad Thai, now's the time to try. This delicious supper is so satisfying and easy to make. If you don't have any of the falafel burger mixture, you can use other falafel or even shop-bought ones to add to the pad Thai. If you're vegetarian or vegan use a vegan-friendly nam pla.

SERVES 4
PREP 15 MINUTES
COOK 15 MINUTES

1 quantity uncooked Thai Green
    Curry Falafel Burgers mixture
    (see page 54)
groundnut (peanut) oil, for
    shallow-frying

PAD THAI
300g (10½oz) flat rice noodles
    (dried weight)
2 tbsp groundnut (peanut) oil
3 garlic cloves, crushed
2.5cm (1 inch) piece of fresh root
    ginger, diced
8 spring onions (scallions), sliced
1 red bird's-eye chilli, diced
100g (3½oz/1 cup) beansprouts
2 tbsp nam pla (Thai fish sauce)
1 tbsp tamarind paste
juice of ½ lime
2 tbsp brown sugar
60g (2oz/½ cup) crushed roasted
    peanuts
a handful of coriander (cilantro),
    chopped
lime wedges and sweet chilli
    sauce, to serve

Mould the falafel mixture into small balls. Heat enough oil to cover the base of a large non-stick frying pan (skillet) set over a medium heat and fry the falafel, in batches, turning occasionally, for 4–5 minutes, until crisp and golden brown. Remove and drain on kitchen paper (paper towels). Keep warm.

Meanwhile, prepare the rice noodles according to the instructions on the packet.

Heat the oil in a wok or deep frying pan over a medium to high heat. Stir-fry the garlic, ginger, spring onions and chilli for 1 minute.

Add the rice noodles and beansprouts and stir-fry for 1–2 minutes, tossing them lightly. Mix the nam pla, tamarind paste, lime juice and sugar in a bowl and then stir into the wok. Add the falafel.

Divide the mixture among four serving plates. Sprinkle with the roasted peanuts and coriander and serve immediately with lime wedges and sweet chilli sauce.

VARIATIONS
- Use dried chilli flakes instead of a fresh chilli.
- Stir in two beaten eggs after adding the noodles and beansprouts.
- Add some carrot matchsticks or red and yellow (bell) peppers.

CALIFORNIAN SWEET POTATO FALAFEL BURGERS

//

These burgers are oven-baked, but you can shallow-fry them or cook them on an oiled griddle pan instead. In California, mashed avocado is often added to salad dressings and very good it is, too.

SERVES 4
PREP 25 MINUTES
CHILL 30 MINUTES
COOK 15 MINUTES

1 quantity Sweet Potato Falafel
    mixture (see page 28)
olive oil, for brushing
4 ciabatta or seeded burger buns
4 tbsp Hummus (see page 33)
a few salad leaves
Tahini Yoghurt Sauce (see page
    40), for drizzling

CALIFORNIAN AVOCADO SALAD
1 cos (romaine) lettuce, torn
½ red onion, diced
1 red (bell) pepper, deseeded
    and chopped
1 courgette (zucchini), cut into
    strips with a potato peeler
200g (7oz) cherry or baby plum
    tomatoes, halved
1 juicy orange, peeled and sliced
3 tbsp avocado oil
1 tbsp red wine vinegar
juice of ½ lemon
1 garlic clove, crushed
1 avocado, peeled, stoned, mashed
a handful of coriander (cilantro),
    chopped
sea salt and black pepper

Preheat the oven to 200°C (180°C fan)/400°F/gas 6.

Chill the falafel mixture in the fridge for at least 30 minutes to firm it up. Divide into four portions and, using your hands, mould each one into a burger shape. Place on a lightly oiled baking tray (cookie sheet) and bake in the oven for 15 minutes, or until crisp and golden brown.

Meanwhile, make the salad: put the lettuce, red onion, red pepper, courgette, tomatoes and orange in a large bowl. Whisk the avocado oil, vinegar and lemon juice until well blended and stir in the garlic and mashed avocado. Season to taste and use as a dressing for the salad, tossing everything gently until coated. Sprinkle with coriander.

Split the ciabatta or burger buns and, if wished, toast lightly. Spread the bases with the Hummus and top with salad leaves. Add the cooked burgers and drizzle with Tahini Yoghurt Sauce. Cover with the tops and serve immediately with the salad.

VARIATIONS
- Add some dried chilli flakes or diced sun-blush tomatoes to the salad.
- Drizzle the burgers with Tzatziki (see page 38) or some hot sauce.
- Use olive oil instead of avocado oil.

FALAFEL WITH SPICED CREAMY ONION SAUCE

//

When the weather is cool, try serving your favourite falafel in a gently spiced creamy sauce. Cook the falafel of your choice, or reheat some leftover or bought ones. This is comfort food at its best.

SERVES 4
PREP 15 MINUTES
COOK 15 MINUTES

1 quantity cooked falafel of
    your choice
3 tbsp olive oil
2 large onions, thinly sliced
1 leek, washed, trimmed and
    thinly sliced
1 tsp ground turmeric
1 tsp ground coriander
a pinch of cayenne pepper or
    hot paprika
300g (10½oz) small broccoli
    florets and cut stalks
90ml (3fl oz/scant ½ cup) boiling
    vegetable stock
240ml (8fl oz/1 cup) crème
    fraîche
a squeeze of lemon juice
sea salt and freshly ground
    black pepper
cooked rice or pasta, to serve

Make and cook the falafel according to the instructions in the recipe.

Meanwhile, heat the olive oil in a large non-stick frying pan (skillet) over a medium heat. Add the onion and leek and cook, stirring occasionally, for 8–10 minutes or until really tender, golden brown and starting to caramelize. Stir in the spices and cook for 1 minute.

Add the broccoli florets and boiling stock. Cover the pan and cook for about 4 minutes, until the broccoli is starting to soften but still retains a little bite. Add the crème fraîche and a squeeze of lemon juice and season to taste.

Add the hot falafel and serve in the pool of creamy sauce with some pasta or steamed or boiled rice.

VARIATIONS
· Serve with quinoa or couscous.
· Sprinkle with toasted pine nuts.
· Cook some grated fresh root ginger with the onions and leek.
· Use reduced-fat crème fraîche instead of full fat.
· Substitute asparagus, cut into 2.5cm (1 inch) lengths, for the broccoli.
· Or stir some shredded spinach into the fried onions and leek.
· Use soured cream instead of crème fraîche.

MEDITERRANEAN FALAFEL BAKE

///

One-pan meals, baked in the oven while you relax and put your feet up, always make the easiest suppers. To make this more substantial you can serve it with some brown rice, quinoa, couscous, freekeh or bulgur wheat.

SERVES 4
PREP 10 MINUTES
COOK 25–30 MINUTES

1 quantity cooked falafel of
   your choice
500g (1lb 2oz) baby carrots,
   trimmed and halved lengthways
2 x 400g (14oz) tins (3 cups)
   chickpeas (garbanzo beans),
   rinsed and drained
3 tbsp olive oil
1 tsp cumin seeds
1 tsp crushed coriander seeds
1 tbsp mixed sunflower and
   flax seeds
400g (14oz) cherry tomatoes
300g (10½oz) kale or spinach,
   washed, trimmed and roughly
   shredded
a handful of flat-leaf parsley,
   chopped
Tahini Yoghurt Sauce (see page
   40), for drizzling
sea salt and freshly ground
   black pepper

Make and cook the falafel according to the instructions in the recipe.

Preheat the oven to 190°C (170°C fan)/375°F/gas 5.

Put the carrots and chickpeas in a large roasting pan and drizzle with the olive oil. Sprinkle the seeds over the top and season with salt and pepper.

Bake in the preheated oven for 15 minutes. Add the cherry tomatoes and kale or spinach and stir into the seedy oil. Place the falafel on top and bake for another 10–15 minutes or until the vegetables are tender and the falafel are heated through and golden brown.

Sprinkle with parsley and check the seasoning, then divide among four serving plates. Drizzle with Tahini Yoghurt Sauce and serve hot or warm.

VARIATIONS
- Use parsnips, sweet potatoes, pumpkin or squash.
- Add some feta cheese or creamy Taleggio or Gorgonzola at the end.
- Sprinkle with spicy dukkah.
- Serve with Tzatziki (see page 38) or even guacamole.
- Substitute other herbs such as mint, basil or coriander (cilantro) for the parsley.

QUINOA AND MANGO FALAFEL BOWL

//

This meal in a bowl is so healthy – it's full of vegetable protein, high in fibre and gluten-free. You can use any leftovers in a lunchbox for tomorrow. You can use any falafel, freshly made or reheated.

SERVES 4
PREP 20 MINUTES
COOK 30 MINUTES

1 quantity cooked falafel of
    your choice
2 red or yellow (bell) peppers,
    deseeded and cut into chunks
1 red onion, cut into wedges
2 raw beetroot (beets), peeled
    and cut into small wedges
4 garlic cloves, unpeeled
4 tbsp olive oil
480ml (16floz/2 cups) vegetable
    stock
200g (7oz/scant 1¼ cups) quinoa
    (dried weight), rinsed and
    drained
1 ripe mango, peeled, stoned
    (pitted) and cubed
1 ripe avocado, peeled, stoned
    (pitted) and cubed
toasted pine nuts, for sprinkling
Tahini Yoghurt Sauce (see page
    39), for drizzling
sea salt and black pepper

DRESSING
3 tbsp olive oil
juice of 1 lemon
2 tsp sumac
a pinch of sugar
a few sprigs of cilantro
    (coriander), finely chopped

Make and cook the falafel according to the instructions in the recipe.

Preheat the oven to 200°C (180°C fan)/400°F/gas 6.

Put the peppers, red onion and beets into a large roasting pan. Tuck the garlic in between and drizzle with olive oil. Turn the vegetables in the oil to coat them and season. Roast in the preheated oven for 25–30 minutes, or until tender. Squeeze the garlic out of the skins and mix in to the vegetables.

Meanwhile, bring the stock to the boil in a saucepan, tip in the quinoa and reduce the heat to a simmer. Cover and cook for 15 minutes or until the quinoa is tender and has absorbed most of the stock. When it's cooked, the sprout or 'tail' will pop out of each seed. Remove from the heat and stand for 5 minutes before straining and fluffing up with a fork.

Make the dressing: whisk the ingredients with the oil from the vegetables.

Put the quinoa, mango and avocado in a bowl and toss in the dressing. Divide among four shallow serving bowls and top with the hot falafel. Spoon the roasted vegetables into the bowls and serve sprinkled with toasted pine nuts and drizzled with Tahini Yoghurt Sauce.

VARIATIONS
· Serve with Quick-and-easy Hummus (see page 33),
  Tzatziki (see page 38), harissa or hot sauce.
· Fold in some baby spinach leaves or shredded kale.
· Add some cubed feta or griddled sliced halloumi.
· Use roasted pumpkin, squash, carrot, courgettes
  (zucchini) or aubergine (eggplant).
· Sprinkle with toasted seeds or dukkah.

WRAPS, SANDWICHES AND SNACKS

SESAME GREEN FALAFEL AND TOFU FLATBREADS

//

You can make these delicious flatbreads with your favourite green falafel from the basics chapter. When you make up the recipe, roll or sprinkle the uncooked falafel with sesame seeds before frying or baking them. Vegans can use non-dairy yoghurt.

SERVES 4
PREP 15 MINUTES
COOK 10 MINUTES

1 quantity cooked green falafel of
    your choice
sesame seeds, for sprinkling
300g (10½oz) extra-firm or firm
    tofu, cubed
olive oil, for brushing
4 large flatbreads
8 heaped tbsp Quick-and-easy
    Hummus (see page 33)
1 ripe avocado, peeled, stoned
    (pitted) and sliced
a handful of coriander (cilantro),
    chopped
dried chilli flakes or hot sauce
    (optional)

MINT TAHINI YOGHURT SAUCE
240g (8½oz/1 cup) Greek
    yoghurt
3 tbsp tahini
2 garlic cloves, crushed
grated zest and juice of ½ lemon
a handful of mint, finely chopped
sea salt and freshly ground
    black pepper

Make and cook the falafel according to the instructions in the recipe, sprinkling them with sesame seeds before cooking.

Make the mint tahini yoghurt sauce: put all the ingredients in a bowl and beat together until smooth and well combined. The sauce will be quite thick, so add enough cold water to thin it to the consistency you desire.

Season the tofu with salt and pepper. Lightly brush a large ridged griddle pan with oil and place over a medium heat. When it's hot, add the tofu and cook for about 5 minutes, turning occasionally, until crisp and golden brown all over. Remove and drain on kitchen paper (paper towels).

Warm the flatbreads in the hot griddle pan or in a low oven. Spread each flatbread with 2 heaped tablespoons Hummus and put the avocado, hot falafel and tofu on top. Sprinkle with the coriander and drizzle with the mint tahini yoghurt sauce. Top with a sprinkle of chilli flakes or some hot sauce, if using.

Place each flatbread on a square of foil or baking parchment and fold up or roll over to enclose the filling. Eat immediately while they are still warm.

VARIATIONS
- Drizzle with Lemony Green Tahini Sauce (see page 41).
- Use guacamole instead of a sliced avocado.
- Add some bottled roasted red and yellow (bell) peppers.
- Add some chopped sun-blush or sun-dried tomatoes.

HALLOUMI FALAFEL PITA POCKETS

///

Traditional Falafel (see page 14) are perfect in these cheesy pita pockets, but you can use any of the falafel in the basic recipe section. Halloumi is great for pitas and wraps as its high melting point means that it keeps its shape and won't melt on a griddle pan, grill (broiler) or barbecue.

SERVES 4
PREP 15 MINUTES
COOK 5 MINUTES

1 quantity cooked falafel of
    your choice
250g (9oz) halloumi cheese,
    sliced
olive oil for shallow frying
4 large pita breads
a handful of salad leaves
12 baby plum tomatoes, halved
½ red onion, thinly sliced
4 heaped tbsp Tzatziki (see
    page 38)
sea salt and freshly ground
    black pepper

Make and cook the falafel according to the instructions in the recipe.

Heat a lightly oiled ridged griddle pan over a medium heat and add the halloumi, a few slices at a time. Cook for 2–3 minutes each side or until crisp, golden brown and attractively striped. Remove and drain on kitchen paper (paper towels).

Meanwhile, toast the pita breads or warm them on a lightly oiled griddle pan. Make a slit down one side of each pita and open it.

Fill the warm pitas with the salad leaves, tomatoes and red onion. Cover with the halloumi and hot falafel. Season with salt and pepper and top with Tzatziki. Serve immediately while the falafel and halloumi are warm.

Tip: This is a good way of using up leftover falafel. Just reheat them in the oven and add to the pita pockets.

VARIATIONS
- Use Quick-and-easy Hummus (see page 33) instead of the Tzatziki.
- Top with a spoonful of Greek yoghurt and a dash of harissa paste.
- Drizzle with Tahini Yoghurt Sauce (see page 40) or Lemony Green Tahini Sauce (see page 41).
- Drizzle with sweet chilli sauce or sriracha.
- Add some sliced avocado.
- Add some roasted or griddled vegetables, e.g. (bell) peppers, aubergine (eggplant) and mushrooms.

FALAFEL SOUVLAKI

//

Greek souvlaki are traditionally made with grilled meat, wrapped up with salad and fried potatoes in a thick, soft flatbread. But you can make this wonderful vegan version with your favourite falafel and griddled aubergine (eggplant).

SERVES 4
PREP 20 MINUTES
COOK 15–20 MINUTES

1 quantity cooked falafel of
    your choice
2 aubergines (eggplants), thickly
    sliced
olive oil, for brushing
1 tsp za'atar
1 tsp dried oregano
4 large thick flatbreads
crisp lettuce leaves, shredded
4 tomatoes, quartered
½ red onion, thinly sliced
Skordalia (see page 34)
1–2 tsp harissa paste
lemon wedges, for squeezing
sea salt and freshly ground
    black pepper

Make and cook the falafel according to the instructions in the recipe.

Lightly brush the aubergines on both sides with oil. Sprinkle with the za'atar and oregano and season with salt and pepper.

Place a large ridged griddle pan over a medium to high heat and, when it's hot, add the aubergine in batches. Cook for 2–3 minutes each side, or until golden brown and starting to char. Drain on kitchen paper (paper towels) and keep warm.

Warm the flatbreads in a low oven or on a lightly oiled griddle pan. Arrange the lettuce, tomatoes and onion on top and then add the aubergine and hot falafel. Season with salt and pepper and top with the Skordalia and a little harissa.

Place each flatbread on a square of foil or baking parchment and fold up or roll over to enclose the filling. Eat immediately while they are warm with some lemon wedges for squeezing.

VARIATIONS
- Top with Quick-and-easy Hummus (see page 33) or Tzatziki (see page 38) instead of Skordalia.
- Drizzle with Tahini Yoghurt Sauce (see page 40) or Lemony Green Tahini Sauce (see page 41).
- Add some hot sauce.
- Substitute griddled peppers for the aubergine.
- Add some fried or griddled sliced tofu.

FALAFEL BANH MI

//

This Thai snack is similar to the Provençal *pan bagnat* as the soft centre of the baguette is removed and only the shell is used to hold the spicy filling. If you don't have small individual baguettes just buy a long one and cut it into sections. If you can't find vegan nam pla, use soy sauce instead.

SERVES 4
PREP 20 MINUTES
MARINATE 1 HOUR
COOK 5 MINUTES

1 quantity cooked falafel of
    your choice
sesame seeds, for sprinkling
2 carrots, cut into thin
    matchsticks
4 radishes, thinly sliced
1 red (bell) pepper, deseeded
    and thinly sliced
1 small ridged cucumber, cut into
    thin matchsticks
4 tbsp rice vinegar
4 tbsp caster (superfine) sugar
1 tbsp vegan nam pla (Thai fish
    sauce)
4 small baguettes (French sticks),
    halved and hollowed out
1 small red onion, thinly sliced
a handful of mint or basil, chopped
lime wedges, for squeezing

FOR THE HOT MAYO
120g (4oz/½ cup) vegan
    mayonnaise
2 spring onions (scallions), diced
juice of ½ lime
1 tbsp hot sauce, e.g. Sriracha or
    sweet chilli sauce

Make and cook the falafel according to the instructions in the recipe, sprinkling them with sesame seeds before cooking.

Make the hot mayo: mix all the ingredients together in a bowl. Cover and chill in the fridge until needed.

Put the carrots, radishes, red pepper and cucumber in a glass bowl. Heat the vinegar and sugar in a small pan, stirring gently until the sugar dissolves. Bring to the boil and immediately remove from the heat. Stir in the nam pla and pour over the vegetables. Set aside to marinate for at least 1 hour.

Split the baguettes in half lengthways and scoop out some of the soft bread inside to leave a crusty shell. Spread the hot mayo over the bases and then add the falafel (hot or cold), marinated vegetables and the sliced red onion and herbs. Cover with the baguette tops, pressing down firmly, and eat immediately with the lime wedges for squeezing.

VARIATIONS
· Use sliced Japanese daikon instead of radishes.
· Add some pickled chillies or thinly sliced jalapeño.
· Sprinkle with chopped coriander (cilantro).
· Non vegetarians can use regular nam pla (Thai fish sauce).

GREEK SPINACH AND FETA FALAFEL BITES

///

When you bite into these delicious green falafel, there's a hidden surprise – a cube of salty feta cheese. They make great snacks or party canapés served with a bowl of Tzatziki (see page 38). Vegans can serve with Hummus (see page 33) or drizzle with a tahini sauce made from dairy-free yoghurt.

MAKES APPROX. 20 BITES
SOAK OVERNIGHT
PREP 20 MINUTES
CHILL 1–2 HOURS (OPTIONAL)
COOK 10–15 MINUTES

300g (10½oz/generous 1¼ cups) chickpeas (garbanzo beans) (dried weight)
60g (2oz/generous 1 cup) washed, trimmed and shredded spinach
4 spring onions (scallions), chopped
a bunch of flat-leaf parsley, chopped
a handful of mint, chopped
2 garlic cloves, crushed
1½ tbsp chickpea (gram) flour
1 tsp baking powder
1 tsp sea salt
1 tsp ground cumin
1 tsp ground coriander
120g (4oz) feta cheese, cubed
sunflower or vegetable oil, for frying
Tahini Yoghurt Sauce (see page 40), for drizzling
freshly ground black pepper

Put the chickpeas in a large bowl and cover with at least twice as much cold water. You will need plenty as the chickpeas swell and double in size. Leave to soak overnight. The following day, drain the chickpeas and pat dry with kitchen paper (paper towels).

Tip the chickpeas into a food processor and blitz with the spinach, spring onions, herbs and garlic. Add the chickpea flour, baking powder, salt and spices. Pulse, scraping down the sides of the processor occasionally, until finely chopped and the mixture holds together. If it's too dry, add 2–3 tablespoons cold water. Add a good grinding of black pepper and blitz again. Do not over-process – the texture should be grainy, not smooth.

Take a spoonful of the falafel mixture and flatten it with your hands. Put a feta cube in the centre and mould the mixture around it into a small ball. Repeat with the remaining mixture. If wished, cover them and chill in the fridge for 1–2 hours until you're ready to cook. This will help them to firm up.

Pour the oil into a deep heavy-based saucepan to a depth of at least 7.5cm (3in). Place over a medium to high heat and when the temperature reaches 180°C (350°F) (use a sugar thermometer to check), add the falafel, a few at a time, being careful not to overcrowd the pan. Fry for 4–5 minutes until crisp and golden brown all over, then remove with a slotted spoon and drain on kitchen paper (paper towels).

Serve piping hot, drizzled with the Tahini Yoghurt Sauce.

VARIATIONS
· Use cubed halloumi instead of feta.
· Substitute chopped dill for the mint.

SPICY VEGAN FALAFEL SANDWICHES

//

These Lebanese pita sandwiches are really easy to make and you can use freshly cooked or reheated falafel. Make these sandwiches before you leave home in the morning and take them to work or college in a sealed container for a delicious packed lunch. They also taste good served cold.

SERVES 4
PREP 20 MINUTES
COOK 8–16 MINUTES

1 quantity cooked falafel of
  your choice
sesame seeds, for sprinkling
olive oil spray
4 pita breads
100g (3½oz) pickled chillies or
  cucumbers, thinly sliced
Tahini Yoghurt Sauce (see page
  40) made with dairy-free
  yoghurt

LEBANESE SALAD
1 Little Gem lettuce, shredded
2 ripe large plum tomatoes, diced
½ red onion, diced
a handful of mint, chopped
juice of 1 lemon
olive oil, for drizzling
sea salt and freshly ground
  black pepper

Make and cook the falafel according to the instructions in the recipe, sprinkling them with sesame seeds before cooking.

Make the Lebanese salad: mix the lettuce, tomatoes, onion and mint together in a bowl. Squeeze some lemon juice over the top and drizzle with oil. Season with salt and pepper and toss gently.

Heat a griddle pan or large non-stick frying pan (skillet) over a medium to high heat. Lightly spray with olive oil and warm the pitas, one at a time, for 1–2 minutes each side until they start to brown and crisp a little.

Split the pitas open down one side and fill with the salad, pickled chillies or cucumbers and hot falafel. Drizzle with the Tahini Yoghurt Sauce and eat immediately.

VARIATIONS
· Add some sliced bright pink Lebanese pickled turnips.
· Add some harissa paste or hot sauce.
· Stir some diced avocado into the salad.
· Roll up the filling in a wrap or flatbread.
· Add some Hummus (see page 33) or garlic sauce.
· Serve with some Labneh (see page 35).
· Use coriander (cilantro) or flat-leaf parsley instead of mint.

MEXICAN FALAFEL FAJITA WRAPS

//

Adding falafel to vegetable fajitas is not as strange as it sounds. They complement each other perfectly and taste delicious. Vegans can serve them with vegan-friendly soured cream or dairy-free yoghurt.

SERVES 4
PREP 20 MINUTES
COOK 10 MINUTES

1 quantity cooked falafel of
   your choice
olive oil, for brushing
2 large red onions, thinly sliced
2 red or green (bell) peppers,
   deseeded and thinly sliced
2 garlic cloves, thinly sliced
200g (7oz/generous 1 cup)
   tinned black beans, rinsed
   and drained
8 large flour or corn tortilla wraps
a few crisp cos (romaine) lettuce
   leaves, shredded
a handful of coriander (cilantro),
   roughly chopped
Lemony Green Tahini Sauce (see
   page 41), for drizzling
sea salt and freshly ground
   black pepper
soured cream and guacamole,
   to serve

Make and cook the falafel according to the instructions in the recipe. Cut them in half unless they are flat patty-shaped ones.

Lightly brush a large non-stick ridged griddle pan with oil and set over a medium to high heat. Add the red onion, peppers and garlic and cook for 6–8 minutes, turning occasionally, until tender, slightly charred and the onion is starting to caramelize. Remove from the pan, season with salt and pepper and stir in the black beans. Keep warm.

Put the tortillas in the hot pan – just long enough to warm them through. Or you can warm them in the microwave or wrapped in foil in a low oven.

Divide the lettuce and coriander among the warm tortillas. Top with the falafel and the pepper, onion and bean mixture. Drizzle with the tahini sauce and roll up the tortillas. Eat immediately with soured cream and guacamole.

VARIATIONS
· Add some diced avocado or tinned sweetcorn kernels.
· Drizzle with hot sauce or add some shredded hot chilli.
· Sprinkle with grated cheese before rolling the tortillas.
· Use lime juice instead of lemon in the tahini sauce.
· Serve with a fresh hot tomato salsa.

FALAFEL SCOTCH EGGS

///

These are perfect for packed lunches, picnics and snacks. If you're making falafel, try making double the quantity of uncooked mixture and save half for these veggie Scotch eggs. Keep in an airtight container in the fridge for up to three days. You can coat the Scotch eggs with breadcrumbs or panko, but it's not essential.

MAKES 6 SCOTCH EGGS
PREP 30 MINUTES
COOK 20–25 MINUTES

7 medium free-range eggs
1 quantity uncooked Really Green Falafel mixture (see page 15)
plain (all-purpose) flour, for dusting
dried breadcrumbs or panko, for coating (optional)
sunflower or vegetable oil, for frying
Tahini Yoghurt Sauce (see page 40), to serve

VARIATIONS

- Use the Traditional falafel mixture (see page 14) and add a beaten egg.
- Add some sesame seeds to the breadcrumbs or panko before coating.
- Serve with tomato ketchup, chilli sauce, mayonnaise or Tzatziki (see page 38).

Put six of the eggs in a large saucepan and cover with cold water. Bring to the boil and cook for 5 minutes. Remove the eggs with a slotted spoon and plunge them into a bowl of cold water. When they are cool enough to handle, peel away the shells.

Beat the remaining egg in a jug and stir into the uncooked falafel mixture. If it's too dry, add a little water to moisten it; if it's too wet and sticky, stir in a little flour. Divide the mixture into six portions. Flatten each portion into a thin round either with your hands or by rolling out with a rolling pin.

Dust the peeled eggs with flour and gently shake off any excess. Place an egg on one of the falafel rounds and wrap the mixture around the egg, so it is completely covered. Gently squeeze the joins together to seal the egg inside. Repeat with the remaining mixture and eggs. If wished, you can roll the covered eggs in dried breadcrumbs or panko to coat them.

Pour enough oil into a deep heavy-based saucepan to come halfway up the sides. Place over a medium to high heat and when the temperature reaches 180°C (350°F) (use a sugar thermometer to check), add the eggs, two or three at a time, depending on the size of the pan. Fry for 4–5 minutes, turning once or twice, until crisp and golden brown all over. Remove carefully with a slotted spoon and drain on kitchen paper (paper towels).

Serve the Scotch eggs warm or cold, cut in half and drizzled with the Tahini Yoghurt Sauce.

Tip: Use a deep-fat fryer if you have one to cook the falafel Scotch eggs.

HALLOUMI AND FALAFEL GREEK SALAD WRAPS

//

A simple Greek salad, griddled crisp halloumi and falafel make a delicious combo in a wrap. It's a filling snack or a healthy lunch, especially in summer. You can use any falafel, hot or cold.

SERVES 4
PREP 20 MINUTES
COOK 5 MINUTES

1 quantity cooked falafel of
   your choice
225g (8oz) halloumi cheese,
   sliced
olive oil, for brushing
1 tsp dried oregano
4 large flour tortilla wraps
1 cos (romaine) lettuce, shredded
2 bottled roasted red (bell)
   peppers, drained and thinly
   sliced
¼ cucumber, cut into matchsticks
175g (6oz) baby plum tomatoes,
   halved
¼ red onion, thinly sliced
12 black olives, stoned (pitted)
120ml (4fl oz/½ cup) Tzatziki
   (see page 38)

GREEK DRESSING
2 tbsp fruity extra-virgin olive oil
1 tbsp red wine vinegar
a squeeze of lemon juice
a pinch of dried oregano
sea salt and freshly ground black
   pepper

Make and cook the falafel according to the instructions in the recipe.

Make the Greek dressing by whisking all the ingredients together and set aside until needed.

Brush the halloumi slices with oil and sprinkle with oregano. Heat a ridged griddle pan and cook the halloumi over a medium heat for 1–2 minutes each side until striped and golden. Remove and drain on kitchen paper (paper towels).

Warm the tortilla wraps on the hot griddle pan or in a low oven.

Toss the lettuce, peppers, cucumber, tomatoes, onion and olives in the Greek dressing and divide among the wraps. Top with the falafel and halloumi, then drizzle with Tzatziki.

Fold over or roll up the wraps and eat immediately while the halloumi is hot.

VARIATIONS
· Omit the halloumi and add diced feta cheese to
  the salad.
· Add some cubed avocado and chopped parsley or
  coriander (cilantro).
· Sprinkle with dried chilli flakes.
· Drizzle with hot sauce or pomegranate molasses.
· Add some cooked chicken or lamb.
· Use Quick-and-easy Hummus (see page 33) or plain
  yoghurt instead of tzatziki.

FALAFEL, CRUNCHY CARROT AND HUMMUS WRAP

//

Everyone loves wraps... they're healthy, nutritious, quick and easy to make, and good for eating on the go. We've used seedy red onion and crunchy carrots to complement the grainy hummus and spicy falafel. Vegans can use dairy-free yoghurt.

SERVES 4
PREP 15 MINUTES
COOK 8 MINUTES

1 quantity cooked falafel of
   your choice
2 tbsp extra-virgin olive oil
1 small red onion, thinly sliced
4 large carrots, peeled and cut
   into matchsticks
3 garlic cloves, crushed
1 red bird's eye chilli, diced
1 tsp caraway seeds
1 tsp cumin seeds
4 large flour tortilla wraps
200g (7oz/scant 1 cup)
   Quick-and-easy Hummus
   (see page 33)
4 heaped tbsp Greek yoghurt
a large handful of coriander
   (cilantro), chopped
sweet chilli sauce, for drizzling
sea salt and freshly ground
   black pepper

Make and cook the falafel according to the instructions in the recipe.

Heat the olive oil in a large non-stick frying pan (skillet) over a medium heat. Add the onion, carrots, garlic, chilli and seeds and cook, stirring occasionally, for 8 minutes, or until the onion softens and the carrot is tender but still retains some crunch. Season with salt and pepper.

Warm the tortilla wraps on a hot griddle pan or in a low oven.

Spread the Hummus over the tortillas and pile the seedy carrot mixture and the falafel on top. Add the yoghurt and sprinkle with coriander. Drizzle with chilli sauce, roll up and enjoy.

VARIATIONS
· Add some Tzatziki (see page 38) or Baba Ghanoush (see page 79).
· Sprinkle with chopped flat-leaf parsley or dill.
· Add some black mustard seeds or fennel seeds.
· Add some leftover shredded roast chicken.

TOASTED FALAFEL AND MOZZARELLA CIABATTA

///

We've used olive oil and vegan cheese to make these toasties vegan friendly, but you can substitute butter and regular sliced mozzarella. If you have a sandwich toaster, you can oil or butter the ciabatta liberally and toast them. Or try cooking them on a hot ridged griddle pan until striped, crispy and golden brown.

SERVES 4
PREP 10 MINUTES
COOK 8–10 MINUTES

½ quantity cooked falafel of
    your choice
4 ciabatta rolls
olive oil spray
4 heaped tbsp red pesto
a handful of rocket (arugula)
200g (7oz/2 cups) grated vegan
    mozzarella
tomato ketchup or sweet chilli
    sauce, to serve

Make and cook the falafel according to the instructions in the recipe. If the falafel are not flat patty-shaped ones, cut them in half.

Cut each ciabatta in half and spray the outsides lightly with olive oil. Turn them over, inside crumb-up, and spread the four bases with the red pesto. Top with the rocket and falafel and sprinkle the grated mozzarella over the top. Cover with the ciabatta 'lids'.

Spray a large non-stick frying pan (skillet) with oil and set over a medium heat. When it's hot, add the filled ciabatta rolls and cook for 4–5 minutes each side until golden brown and the mozzarella has melted and is oozing.

Serve piping hot with some ketchup or sweet chilli sauce on the side.

VARIATIONS
- Use focaccia rolls or plain sliced sourdough bread.
- Spread with green pesto, sun-dried tomato paste or tapenade.
- Any grated vegan hard cheese will work well.
- Add some dried chilli flakes, harissa or chopped sun-blush tomatoes.
- Serve with some Quick-and-easy Hummus (see page 33) or Tzatziki (see page 38).

ONION BHAJI AND FALAFEL WRAPS

///

You can eat these wraps hot or cold – they taste amazing either way and are great for using up leftover falafel or bhajis. Vegans can use dairy-free yoghurt.

SERVES 4
PREP 25 MINUTES
COOK 15 MINUTES

½ quantity cooked falafel of
  your choice
4 large naan flatbreads or
  chapatis
2 handfuls of crisp lettuce,
  shredded
4 tomatoes, sliced
4 tbsp mango chutney
natural yoghurt, for drizzling

ONION BHAJIS
100g (3½oz/1¼ cups) chickpea
  (gram) flour
½ tsp baking powder
1 tbsp melted ghee or butter
2 tbsp natural yoghurt
2 garlic cloves, crushed
1 tsp cumin seeds
½ tsp ground turmeric
½ tsp chilli powder
a handful of coriander (cilantro),
  finely chopped
2 onions, halved and thinly sliced
sunflower or vegetable oil, for
  deep-frying

Make and cook the falafel according to the instructions in the recipe.

Make the onion bhajis: put the chickpea flour and baking powder in a large bowl and stir in the melted ghee or butter and yoghurt, plus enough cold water to make a thick batter. Stir in the garlic, cumin seeds, turmeric, chilli powder and coriander. Finally, gently fold in the onions.

Heat the oil for deep-frying in a deep-fat fryer or pour in enough to come to a depth of 7.5cm (3in) in a deep heavy-based saucepan. When it reaches 180°C (350°F) (use a sugar thermometer to check), start adding tablespoons of the onion batter to the hot oil, a few at a time. Cook for 3–4 minutes until crisp and golden. Remove with a slotted spoon and drain on kitchen paper (paper towels).

Warm the naan or chapatis in a low oven or heat them on a griddle pan. Arrange the lettuce and tomatoes on top and add the falafel and bhajis. Top with mango chutney and drizzle with yoghurt. Roll up and eat immediately.

VARIATIONS
· Add some shredded spinach, cucumber or grated carrot.
· Drizzle with cucumber raita or hot chilli sauce.
· Use red onions instead of white ones in the bhajis.

INDEX